GW01403005

INDEX

KIDNAPPING MOUN

STEPPE BY STEPPE ROMANTICS

Ethnolinguistic Groups in the Caucasus Region

Ukraine

Rostov

Rostov

Kazakhstan

Astrakhan'

Sea of Azov

Krasnodar Kray

Elista

Kalmykia

Astrakhan'

Krasnodar

Stavropol'

Adygea

Maykop'

Stavropol' Kray

Russia

Caspian Sea

Cherkessk

Karachay-Cherkessia

Nal'chik

Kabardino-Balkaria

Chechnya

Ingushetia Nazran'

Groznyy

Vladikavkaz

North Ossetia

Dagestan

Makhachkala

Black Sea

K'ut'aisi

South Ossetia

Ts'khinvali

Georgia

T'bilisi

Bat'umi

Armenia

Yerevan

Azerbaijan

Xankändi (Stepanakert) Nagorny-Karabakh

Baku

Naxcivan

Azer.

Naxçıvan (Nakhichevan)

Turkey

Iran

Caucasian Peoples

Abkhaz
1   Abkhaz

Circasian
2   A   Adygey
3   Cherkess
4   Kabardin

Georgian
5   G   Georgian

Dagestani
6   Agul
7   Avar
8   D   Dargin
9   I   Lak
10   L   Lezgin
11   Rutul
12   Tabasaran
13   Tsakhur

Veinakh
14   Chechen
15   Ingush

  Other

Indo-European Peoples

Armenian
16   a   Armenian

Greek
17   Greek

Iranian
18   K   Kurd
19   O   Ossetian
20   Talysh

Slavic
21   R   Russian

Altaic Peoples

Turkic
22   Z   Azeri
23   Balkar
24   Karachay
25   Kumyk
26   Nogay
27   T   Turkmen

Mongol
28   Kalmyk

Sparsely populated or uninhabited areas are shown in white

— Republic, oblast, or kray boundary

0   100 Kilometers
0   100 Miles

Perry-Castañeda Library Map Collection, The University of Texas at Austin Produced by the U.S. Central Intelligence Agency

Prologue

It is a dizzying time for those of us who have lived in the minority. For we are thrust into the unforgiving spotlight of the majority by a pace of events that risks running so far ahead of us that our bodies are all indistinguishable, a huddled mass in the unforgiving rear-view mirror of history.

Distinctions often dismissed with strange delectation – 'obscure', 'minority', or even 'underground' – risk becoming just that if current opportunities to re-engage with both fact and fiction are not confronted head-on. For previously minority suspicions are today menaced by the scope, scale, and activation of *common sense*. Whether it's the minority conviction that complexity is to be harnessed, not dismissed, ignored, or neutered, or the minority stand that, despite an unprecedented bias towards the image, the word still matters, a lot. This *common sense* – be it meaning shared by a collective or an engagement with the reality of the majority – acts as a margin call to the very *raison d'être* of those of us who have, thus far, found a certain elegance in refusal. Nowhere do we witness the need to embrace the majority more critically and urgently than in the brutalist elaboration – of languages, landscape, and lines – better known as the Caucasus.

Coat of arms of South Ossetia adopted May 1998

Ramonov Vano in eighteenth-century Ossetian Northern Caucasian dress North Ossetia state joint museum of history, architecture, and literature

Kidnapping Mountains is an exploration of the Caucasus with a wilful intoxication of the muscular stories, muscular wills, and muscular defeat inhabiting these lands. The book is comprised of two parts: an eponymous section addressing the complexity of languages and identities on the very fault line of Eurasia and *Steppe by Steppe*, a redemption of seemingly reactionary approaches to romance in the greater region.

'Jabal al-alsun', or the 'Mountain of Tongues', is how Al-Mas'udi, a tenth-century Arab geographer, referred to the Caucasus in his *Muruj adh-dhahab wa ma'adin al-jawahir* [*The Meadows of Gold and Mines of Gems*]. Nineteenth-century Russians called it Warm Siberia. Mountain peoples themselves have as many ways as there are peoples (and at last count, there were twenty-six) to describe themselves.

If mountains make men, then they make them strong and almost astoundingly tangled. We often mistake simplicity for a sign of strength, but the Caucasus is every bit an exception to the rule. The mountainous landscape has resulted in a multiplicity of ethnicities, languages, and names that seems as fit for the alternative cosmogony of a science-fiction author as it does for an anthropological study. There are Laks, Lezgins, Circassians, Kabardins, Balkarians, Avarians, and Kulmyks. Not to mention the Dargins, Kists, Aguls, Adyghe, Svans, and Laz. All this before finally coming up for air with more newsworthy, if not necessarily more obvious, peoples such as Georgians, Armenians, Azerbaijanis, Dagestanis, Ingushetians, Chechens, and Ossetians. But beware those who believe we are trading in the obscure. These are the very peoples whose ethno-linguistic origin – that is, Caucasian – is ostensibly the foundation of western civilisation. A civilisation which has of late betrayed its base, to use political currency, and whose remit has been kidnapped, taken from the terrain of intricacy and intimacy to one of reductive simplicity.

Welcome to Ossetia – Alania! ossetians.com

Conference of Circassian princes in 1839-40 from the album *Le Concaseploresque. Dessiné d'apres nature par le Prince G.Gagarin*, Paris, 1847, nartalbum.com

A Russian convoy outside the village of Dzhaba in South Ossetia

With nations existing side-by-side, but isolated linguistically from neighbours only a short distance away, the Caucasus are a testament to the power and complexity of language and geography. Not because of the distance, which separates one nation or people from another, but rather because of the topographic melodrama that captivates them all, whether they number in the millions or just a handful. The inanimate gives the animate a run for its money here: take the Khodori Gorge.[1] Having recently returned to notoriety due to the Russo-Georgian war of August 2008, the Khodori Gorge's primary firewall acted as a wedge of land between two distinct languages: Ossetian, and Georgian, with their respective Iranian and Mingrelian roots. Long before the human race was ever graced with the dyspeptic displeasure of three words in particular succession – military industrial complex – landscape and language did, and continue to wield an impressive arsenal of arms of their own.[2]

For the better part of the last five hundred years, the region has been caught at a crossroads between three Empires – Ottoman, Persian and Russian – not to mention the disproportionately influential outsiders (the British), and the insiders (the Caucasians themselves) if the rich term can be salvaged from its

[1] There are several such examples, from the Georgian Military Road to Mt. Elbruz.

[2] J.C. Catford, 'Mountain of Tongues: The Languages of the Caucasus', *Annual Review of Anthropology*, 1977, no.6, pp. 283-314.

[3] 'For every *sand-nigger* or *camel-jockey* I had to endure throughout my youth, there were an equal number of attempted consolations from my Iranian elders, reassuring me that I was a Caucasian, an Aryan, just like those who had insulted me. Never mind that the word *Aryan* was about as desirable as *Communist* for anyone born, raised, and educated in post-war America; or that *Caucasian* essentially meant *white* and a mere glance in the mirror showed that to be a stretch at best…' Payam Sharifi.

[4] A German scientist and classical anthropologist, Johann Friedrich Blumenbach (1752 – 1840) was responsible for the use of the word Caucasian to mean people originally from the Caucasus, and, in more common parlance, peoples with European heritage. Blumenbach employed the highly dubious study of comparative anatomy and craniology to determine the Caucasian, and in particular, the Georgian, to be 'the most beautiful race of men'.

[5] Including present-day central Armenia, and further parts of Azerbaijan.

Top Row: 1.Nordic (Karl von Müller), 2.Dinaric (Tyrolian woman), 3.Mediterranean (Corsican), 4.Alpine (Heinrich Kiepert)

Bottom Row: 5. East Baltic (Volhynian woman), 6. Turk of Karahissar, 7. Bedouin, 8. Afghan
Meyers 'Blitz-Lexikon', Leipzig,1932

inherent racism.[3] Once upon a time, of course, 'Caucasian' was used as a spuriously academic stand-in for *whitey*.[4]

The Russian state has always looked to the Caucasus as a sunny, if deeply isolated backyard deemed appropriate for a country of Russia's scale. The tug of war between Russia and Persia in the nineteenth century saw the Caucasus veer progressively towards the Russian camp, with two notable milestones: the Treaty of Gulistan in 1813, when Persia gave up Azerbaijan, Dagestan and Georgia, and the Treaty of Turkmenchay in 1828, when further khanates were given up.[5]

We would like to wrest the immanent complexity of the name from its extinguished usage. The Rotring-like precision and subsequent atomisation of peoples and identities makes the history of the Balkans look brush-stroked in comparison. Despite sharing a particular fondness for the multiplicity of languages, cultural affinities, and identities found in the geographic case study called the Caucasus, we wouldn't wish its fractured fate on any people.

Signing of the Treaty of Turkmanchai
opiumandsaffron.blogspot.com

Cheremshah 2007, silver print, 42 x 30 cm

Mikhael
Lermontov

MTSIRI

AND OTHER SELECTED POEMS

Nana Andronikashvili and
Hans von Sachsen-Altenburg
Editors

Mtsiri p. 2

A portion of the proceeds derived from this publication is dedicated to a special fund to obtain wheelchairs and education for children hurt by war activities in Georgia. The fund is also supported by Park Cities Rotary Club, Dallas, Texas, Wheelchair Committee, and District 5810 of Rotary International and matched by The Wheelchair Foundation.

Mtsiri p. 3

Produced with the generous support of
**Business & Engineering Global Outreach –
NHF ("BEGO")**
Jared Michael Jackson, Jr.
Founding Director
Dallas, Texas, and Saratov, Russia

BEGO is a non-profit organisation created to facilitate economic and humanitarian cooperation and development by bringing together people of different nations and cultures. Bego promotes educational programs and cross-cultural expierences to facilitate personal growth and development of personal, business and civic relationships.

Special thanks to
our supporters and partners:
W. David Griggs
Jim Sweitzer
Anastassia Kozlova
Highland Park United Methodist Church
Communities Foundation – Saratov Branch
Saratov United Methodist Church
Communities Foundation of Texas
Fininvest Company
Mary Kay Corporation
Saratov Chamber of Commerce
Dr. Bryan Frank
Dr. & Mrs. Ed Nace
Tricia Holderman
Mr. & Mrs. Jerome Fullinwider
Walt Miller
Lynn Lindsay
Kristall Balalayka

BEGO's proceeds from this book will go toward funding orphanage and school projects in Saratov, Russia.

Mtsiri p. 4

First Edition – 2004
Nana Andronikashvili and
Hans von Sachsen-Altenburg
Editors
ISBN 0-9661902-3-8

Pekitanoui Publications
513 High Street
Boonville, MO 65233
Telephone 660-882-3353

Printed in the United States of America
by Walsworth Publishing Company, Inc.
Marceline, MO 64658

Number _____

Copyright © 2004 Prince Johannes von Sachsen-Altenburg and Princess Nana Andronikashvili von Sachsen-Altenburg

Mtsiri p. 5

History of the English Language Edition of Mtsiri

Mikhael Lermontov
wrote Mtsiri in 1839 while exiled to Georgia.

Vaxtang Eristavi translated Mtsiri in 1955 in Tiflis, Georgia. It was suppressed from publication in 1956. The manuscript was rediscovered in 2002.

Princess Nana Andronikashvili and Prince Hans von Sachsen-Altenburg transcribed and edited it in 2003. This is the first edition of an English translation of Mtsiri.

Published in the United States of America and Tbilisi, Georgia, in 2004.

Mtsiri p. 6

My native soil will not receive
My cold, mute body; and the tale
Of all my bitter pangs will fail
To draw among these walls of stone
Attention to my name unknown.
(Mtsiri, 24.)

The book is dedicated to Peace in the names of Nana's grandfather, Georgian, missing-in-action in the service of the Soviet Union during the first week of May 1945, in or near Berlin, Germany, then 40 years old. Gravesite unknown.

Hans's mother's first husband, German, missing-in-action in the service of the Third Reich of Germany, April 1945, in or near Stalingrad, Russia, then 21 years old. Gravesite unknown.

World War II ended 8 May 1945.

Mtsiri p. 7

Mikhail Yurevich Lermontov was born in Moscow in 1814 and entered Moscow University to study ethics, politics, and literature. In 1932 he was dismissed, reportedly, for disciplinary reasons. Lermontov went to St. Petersburg and graduated from the military school in 1834. The gifted young man began writing poetry at 14 years of age. By 1837 he had already written more than two hundred lyric poems, ten epics and three plays. In that year he wrote a poem Смерть Поета (Smert Poeta) - 'Death of the Poet', dedicated to the death of the great Russian Poet Alexander Pushkin who had been killed in a dual. Смерть Поета (Smert Poeta) made Lermontov famous, but also dangerous to Imperial Russia. Czar Nikolas had him imprisoned and then exiled to the Caucasus region where Lermontov was placed in the Nizhegorodsky Dragon Polk, an elite frontier brigade fighting rebellious mountain tribes and neighboring Turks. Not many soldiers of lower rank survived the constant drill and continuous engagements. Lermontov, however, was luckier than most. He met famous people and was delighted by Georgia's natural beauty.

Lermontov dedicated several poems to Georgia. Although he participated in the Caucasian Wars, he recognized the Caucasian peoples' selfless fight for their independence against the imperialist country he was serving. The exiled revolutionary and displaced soldier-poet sympathized with those fighting for their personal and national freedom.

Mtsiri p. 8

From his earliest studies Lermontov had been inspired by Lord Byron, specifically by his ideas of personal freedom. A good example from the Caucasian period is his party autobiographical work "Hero of Our Times."

Lermontov was exiled to the Caucasus for a second time, on the shores of the Black Sea. He returned to the mountain city of Pyatigorsk for health reasons, where he was killed, like Pushkin, in a dual in 1841, at the age of 27.

Mtsiri takes place in Georgia. The hero is a young prisoner, a Cherkessian boy from a Caucasian tribe fighting for his people's freedom. The poem is a hymn to freedom, homeland and nature.

Russians had always considered the people of Cherkessiato to be dangerous enemies that never abated their struggle for independence and freedom.

Lermontov's words, more than 160 years old, are still quite contemporary today:

Where giddy crags are clad in clouds,
Where men are eagles free and proud.

Mtsiri p. 9

MTSIRI

"I did but taste a little honey,
and, so, I must die."
I Kings

Mtsiri – Georgian, 'a novice on probation in a monastery'.

Mtsiri, first nine acknowledgement pages of the English translation 2004 (opposite)

The *Roublards* and the Restless[1]

There are two types of landmines for the translator: the linguistic one (including connotations, context, usage, or implications) and the factual one. If the former is a garden of delights for the language lothario, the latter is like wrestling with grey on a rainy day.

The bathos of publishers: *Mtsiri* The first English translation of Mikhail Lermontov's *Mtsiri* [The Novice], a poem about a young Caucasian boy adopted by a Russian general and subsequently a monk written in the 1830s, appeared only in 2004.[2] If the introductory pages of the volume are anything to go by, the 170 years or so in between seemed to have been quite eventful. Teeming with intrigue worthy of the Caucasian complexity of its setting – *Mtsiri*'s English translation is also mired in a surreal hotchpotch of Dallas, Saratov, non-profit organisations (read: Highland Park United Methodist Church), corporate sponsorship (read: Mary Kay Cosmetics) and a list of supporters and partners more appropriate for a museum endowed with hundreds of millions of dollars.[3]

We've never shied away from books as monumental edifices (see page 12), but this very slim volume definitely punches above its weight. Whether it's the story of its publishers – a certain Prince Hans von Sachsen-Altenburg and his companion, Princess Nana Andronikasvhili – or that of the translator Vaxtang Eristavi, whose 1955 translation was immediately suppressed and only rediscovered in 2002, one must sift through several pages of bony *how* before finally getting to the meaty *what*.

[1] *Roublard* is an old-fashioned, almost chic, French slang word, referring to a fraudster, derived from the name for the early-twentieth-century Russians who would cheat the French with fraudulent exchange rates between the rouble and the franc.

[2] Mikhail Lermontov, *Mtsiri*, Walsworth Publishing Company, Marceline, 2004.

[3] Hailed as a hero of romanticism throughout Russia, Lermontov is known as the Poet of the Caucasus, due to the respect accorded to him throughout the region. Many of his most important works, including *A Hero of Our Time* (1839/41), were particularly influenced by his time spent there and to this day he enjoys an affection rarely bestowed upon ethnic Russians.

Сон

В полдневный жар в долине Дагестана
С свинцом в груди лежал недвижим я;
Глубокая еще дымилась рана,
По капле кровь точилася моя,
Лежал один я на песке долины;
Уступы скал теснилися кругом,
И солнце жгло их желтые вершины
И жгло меня—но спал я мертвым сном.
И снился мне сияющий огнями
Вечерний пир в родимой стороне.
Меж юных жен, увенчанных цветами,
Шел разговор веселый обо мне.
Но в разговор веселый не вступая,
Сидела там задумчиво одна,
И в грустный сон душа ее младая
Бог знает чем была погружена;
И снилась ей долина Дагестана;
Знакомый труп лежал в долине той;
В его груди, дымясь, чернела рана,
И кровь лилась хладеющей струей.

Tiflis Mikhail Lermontov, 1837

The Dream

In noon's heat, in a dale of Dagestan
With lead inside my breast, stirless I lay;
The deep wound still smoked on; my blood
Kept trickling drop by drop away.
On the dale's sand alone I lay. The cliffs
Crowded around in ledges steep,
And the sun scorched their tawny tops
And scorched me – but I slept death's sleep.
And in a dream I saw an evening feast
That in my native land with bright lights shone;
Among young women crowned with flowers,
A merry talk concerning me went on.
But in the merry talk not joining,
One of them sat there lost in thought,
And in a melancholy dream
Her young soul was immersed – God knows by what.
And of a dale in Dagestan she dreamt;
In that dale lay the corpse of one she knew;
Within his breast a smoking wound showed black,
And blood ran in a stream that colder grew.

The Dream Mikhail Lermontov, 1840, translation Vladimir Nabokov

By turns a historian, an archaeologist, a research fellow at the Southern Methodist University, and head of an oil company, Von Sachsen-Altenburg is both as accomplished and fictitious as his name would leave one to believe. He is wanted for alleged fraud in Georgia and accused of simply adopting the title 'Prince'. Tellingly, his narcissism bleeds into the acknowledgement pages of the English edition of *Mtsiri*, in which the Prince and Princess eclipse the work of its translator with personal tributes to relatives lost in World War II, going so far as to suggest a shameless amalgam of their own relatives' tragedy and that of Lermontov himself, killed a century earlier in 1841 in a duel at the foot of Mount Mashuk, outside Pyatigorsk.

1. Tariel's fight with the lion and the tiger. 2. Tariel at a rocky river. 3. Portrait of Shota Rusthaveli illustrations by S. S. Kobuladze, 1909

The Knight in the Panther's Skin In Marjory Scott Wardrop's translation of Georgia's twelfth-century national epic poem – Shota Rusthaveli's *The Knight in the Panther's Skin* – the beauty in using words as barriers against defeat jumps from the page and illuminates the tricky business of translation. Nobly divorcing the expression from its means, Wardrop chooses 'close rendering' instead of 'translation', 'Attempted by…' instead of the more prosaic 'by…', opting for an old-world elegance in stark contrast to von Sachsen's twenty-first century opportunism.

Marjory Scott Wardrop devoted her life to the study of the Georgian language. She began the translation of *The Knight in the Panther's Skin* in 1891 in Kent and continued to her death in 1909, with a sober deathbed assessment that another ten years would be necessary to properly translate the 1600 quatrains of the original Georgian. Whether you think it's the *Man* or the *Knight* in the Panther's Skin is anyone's guess:[4] we can rest assured the *woman* behind the attempt spent precious hours so that we need not.[5]

[4] See for comparison Shot'ha Rust'haveli, *The Man in the Panther's Skin*, Nekeri, Tbilisi, 2005.

[5] Upon her death, Marjory's brother Sir Oliver Wardrop, a diplomat posted in Tbilisi and a promoter of Georgia's fledgling independence, set up a fund at Oxford University that eventually became the Department of Kartvelian Studies.

ГОР**Ы**Е

ОТ

УМА

ГОРЫ ОТ УМА *(Mountains from Wit)*
ГОРЕ ОТ УМА *(Woe from Wit)* 2009,
wall application

Romancing the Peaks of Polyglots

Armenian versus Georgian The Caucasus have shown to what degree a single, consolidated written language is key to the drafting of a coherent identity. Though plentiful in the region, few languages have made the edifying strides of Armenian or Georgian. Considered to be among the most unique specimens still in active use, each a distinct branch of the Indo-European languages, Armenian and Georgian share, according to one theory, the same founder of their respective alphabets. The monk Saint Mesrop Mashtots (361/2 – 440), who created the Armenian alphabet in the fifth century, would almost certainly have been asked to reflect on the Georgian one as well.

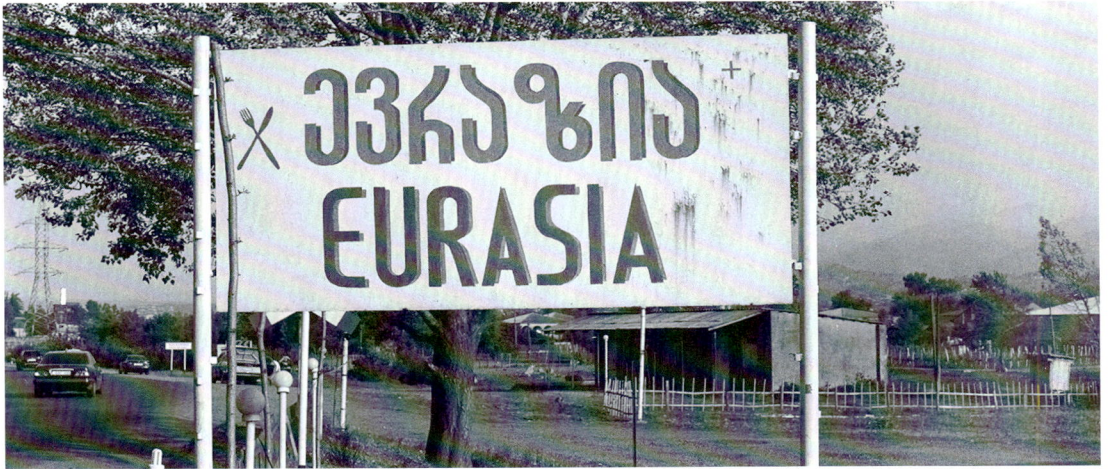

Table of Armenian decorative types by Fred Africkian, Sovetakan Grogh Publishers, Yerevan, 1984 *(opposite)*

Eurasia restaurant sign near Samtredia, Georgia

One joke has it that when Saint Mashtots was done with the Armenian script, he simply threw his plate of pasta onto the wall facing him. As the noodles were slowly sliding down the wall, Mashtots decided to give the Georgian alphabet its curves. Armenian's letters' angles are more geometric, while Georgian letters'

Bathhouse sign Yerevan, Armenia *(left)*

Saint Mesrop Mashtots at the base of Matenadaram ancient manuscripts library, Yerevan, Armenia *(right)*

15

[1] One of many dialects of Adyghe or Circassian: in this case, spoken in the Russian republic of Kabardino-Balkaria.

[2] Quote taken from Yo'av Karny, *Highlanders: A Journey to the Caucasus in Quest of Memory*, Farrar, Straus, and Giroux, New York, 2000, p. 68.

curves are almost baroque. In a region with such oversized ambitions, one can imagine how much the Armenians pride themselves on their script's seniority.

Circassian versus the rest of the world Zaur Naloyev (1928 –), a founder of the Adyghe Khassa, a Circassian grand assembly in Nalchik, the capital of Kabardino-Balkaria, has been fighting a battle to revive the plight of his people. One of many ethnic groups in the north-western Caucasus, the Circassians or 'Adyghe' have been unable to form a collective national identity due to Russia's control of the region since 1864 and their lack of a single, cohesive language. If the Caucasus is known as the 'mountain of languages', then the Circassians form the peak of this plurality, for better and for worse.

Faced with the imminent extinction of the Adyghe language, Naloyev tells a story:

When a child was born to my son, I forbade anyone from speaking to him in Russian or Ossetian or any other language but Kabardin.[1] When I first enrolled him at the kindergarten, he spoke only Kabardin. By the time he finished kindergarten, he spoke a perfect Russian. Now he speaks both. The boy attempts to write novels. When he brought me his first manuscript, I had to bite my tongue. It was a catastrophe for me. The manuscript was written in Russian, in its entirety. In other words, Nalchik has become a factory in which our children are turned into Russians. Russian is a marvelous language. We love it. But when it drives away our hard won language, it becomes our mortal enemy. This is a paradox, but we cannot help it. And this is a tragedy, not only for the Kabardins but for the entire human race. All languages, not only the major ones, are universal treasures. I am delighted that humans have come to recognize the importance of protecting endangered species amongst the plants and the insects and the animals. I had a dream that one day humanity would be wise enough to defend endangered species among languages as well. And I am profoundly disappointed.[2]

Circassian or Adyghe flag designed by David Urquhart (see page 28), still in use today

Adyghe Republic, 1991 circassianworld.com

Zaur Naloyev abazapress.chat.ru

ТИЗИУСХЬАН ИСУС ХРИСТОС

ЕХЬЫЛIЭГЪЭ

КЪЭБАРЫШIУР

(ИНДЖЫЛ)

350078г. Крас...
Христиан...
«АПОКА...ИПС...»

АдыгабзэкIэ

БИБЛИЕР ЗЭЗЫДЗЭКIЫРЭ ИНСТИТУТЫР

1991

Kebarshiur (Indjil) the New Testament in Adyghe,
Institute for Bible Translation, Stockholm, 1991

Traditional Adyghe female costume clow.ru

THE SHORE CLUB

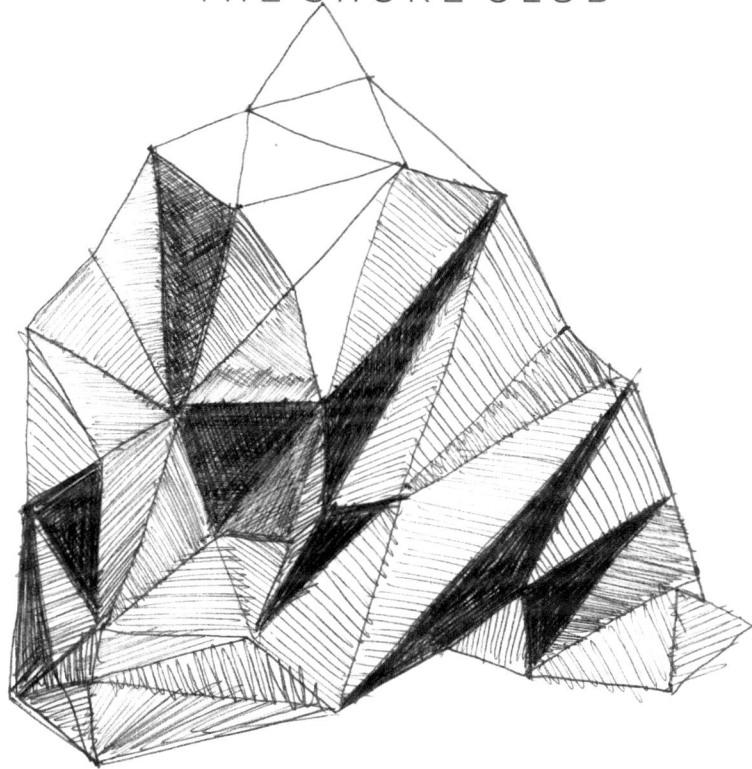

1901 COLLINS AVENUE MIAMI BEACH FLORIDA 33139
PHONE 305 695 3100 FAX 305 695 3299 RESERVATIONS 305 695 3222
SHORECLUB COM

Sketches for Kidnapping Mountains 2009

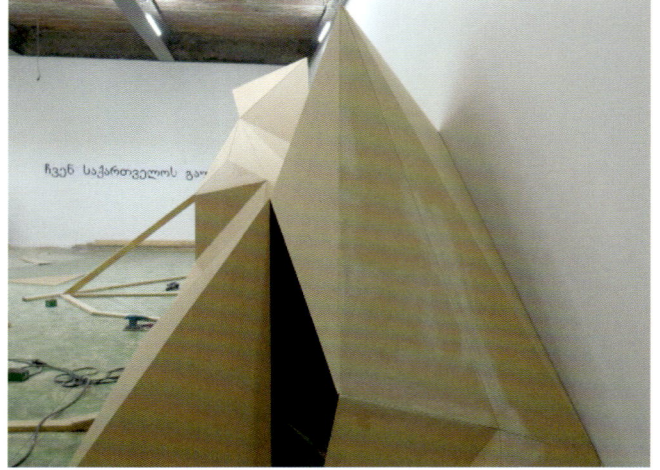

Building of Kidnapping Mountains 2009,
installation, Netwerk, Aalst

Hand-cut mirror mosaics by Gholamhosein Shadizarnagh, 1991 – 2009, Iran
(above and opposite)

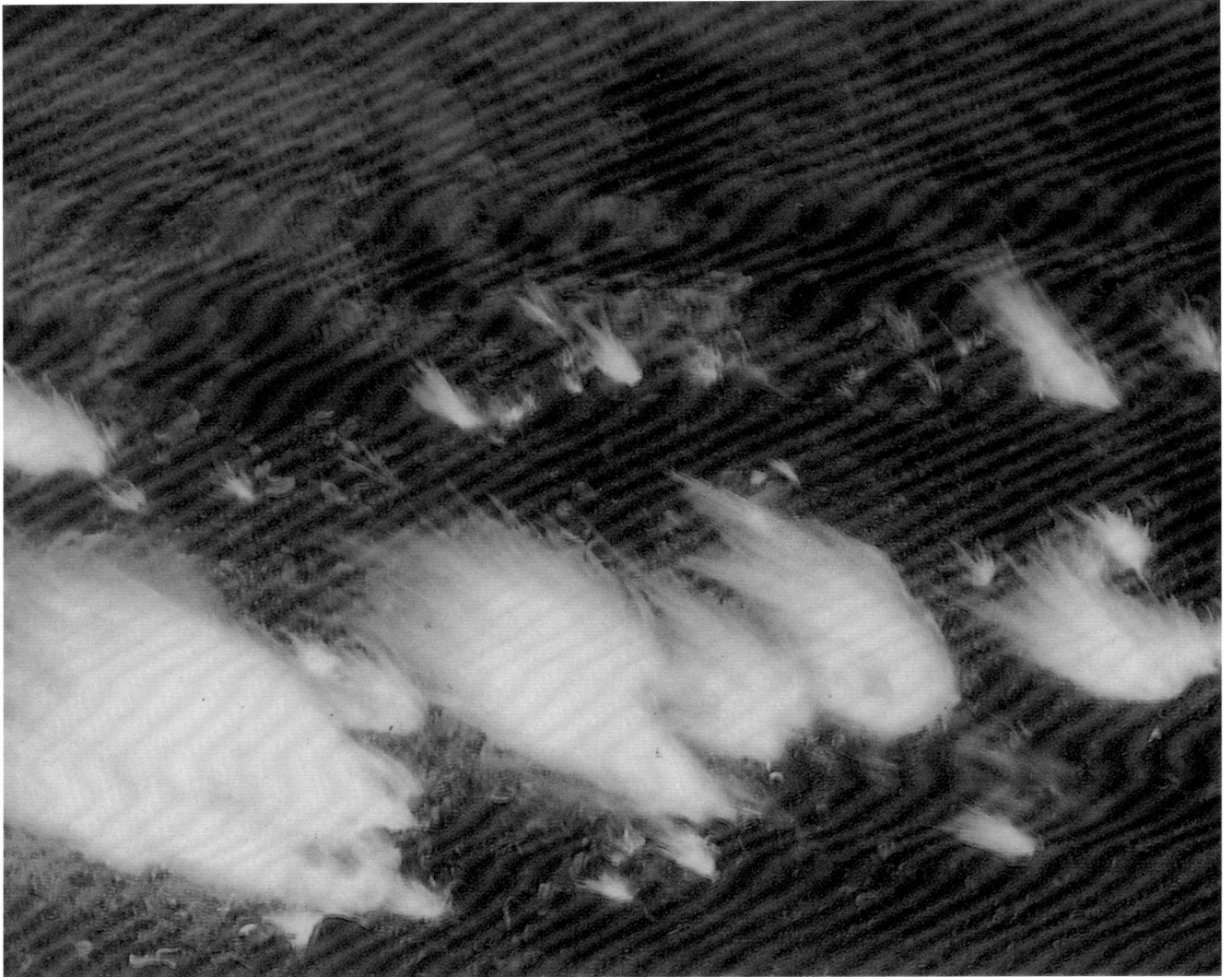

Apsheron Fire, Oil Gusher by G. Guseinzade

Temple of Fire Worshippers Baku, Surakhany, Minaret Publishers, (Author's note: this is most likely a Zoroastrian temple. The Zoroastrians are often mistakenly called fire worshippers)
(left)

Fiery oil columns Baku, Minaret Publishers
(right)

The Broken Men (~~1902~~ 2009)

by Rudyard Aziz Kipling-Khan

For things we never mention,
For nationalism misunderstood –
For excellent intention
That did not turn to good;
From ancient tales' renewing,
From clouds we would not clear –
Beyond the Bolshevik undoing
We fled, and settled here.

We took no tearful leaving,
We bade no long good-byes.
Men talked of drill bits and slaving,
Men wrote of fraud and lies.
To save our injured feelings
'Twas time and time to go –
Behind was dock and Absheron,[1]
Ahead lay Ashghabat![2]

The khânum and the orphan
That pray for ten per cent,
They clapped their trailers on us
To spy the road we went.
They watched the foreign caravans
(They scan the steppes still),
And that's your Jadidi people
Returning good for ill!

God bless the thoughtful islands
Where never warrants come;
God bless the just Republics
That give a khan a home,
That ask no foolish questions,
But set him on his feet;
And save his wife and daughters
From the factory and the street!

On mosque and market
The noonday silence falls;
You'll hear the drowsy mutter
Of the fountain in our squares.
Asleep amidst natural resources

The city takes her ease –
Till twilight brings the land-wind
To the banging double-panes.

Day long the diamond weather,
The high, unaltered blue –
The Turcomans and the sumac
And the barbat tinkling through.
Day long the warder sea
That keeps us from our kin,
And once a month our levee
When the Baku mail comes in.

You'll find us up and waiting
To treat you at the Chai-khâneh;
You'll find us less exclusive
Than your average Cherkess are.
We'll meet you with some horses,
Too glad to show you round,
But – we do not eat the dirty one,
For that is not halal.

We sail o' nights to Azerbaijan
And join our smiling tribes –
Our khânum refrain from advances
And our daughters dance with
Mountain Jews,
But behind our princely doings,
And behind each coup we make,
We feel there's Something Waiting,
And – we meet It when we shake.

Ah, God! One sniff of Baku –
To greet our flesh and blood –
To hear the ships slurring
Once more through petro-gold!
Our towns of wasted honour –
Our streets of lost delight!
How stands old Bibi-Heybat?
Are its waves still ablaze?

[1] The Absheron Peninsula encompasses the Baku metropolitan area as well as Sumqayit. Its name literally means *the place of salty water* in Persian: *ab* meaning water, *shour* meaning salty, and *an,* a suffix denoting the plural.

[2] The capital of Turkmenistan, Ashghabat lies across the Caspian Sea from Baku.

Oil is my shadow. It's what my parents and half of the educated Iranians of the twentieth century studied at university. It's why they settled in Texas, which boasts one of the best petroleum engineering departments in the U.S. at the University of Texas, Austin. It's what fuels the economy of my current home, Russia.

Today it seems the words *oil* and *industry* are dirty words, whose threat grows exponentially the nearer they are to one another. Not only are they considered dirty literally, but, more tellingly, they commit that most heinous of crimes in today's amnesic climate: they recall the *past* (gasp). Cities who see themselves as *modern* only have a historical relationship to the notion of industry and at best a dismissive, albeit disingenuous, left-leaning relationship to oil.

Not Baku, the capital of Azerbaijan. With its past, present and future tenses firmly hinged to petroleum, Baku makes the notion of industry and its urban position not merely relevant, but radically so. The central promenade along the Caspian Sea features an oil well covered in Christmas lights, showing the temperature and time of day. The dusty wells of Bibi-Heybat stand forlornly, a stone's throw from downtown Baku, as a reminder of the fluctuating prices, not to mention the parallel livelihoods of entire populations. And the strangest spot in Baku? Ya-

The Tower with Clock After renovation it was presented to the Azeri people on Nowruz, the 20th of March 2006

Heydər Əliyev Adına Saray, also known as Baku Palace The country's main music venue, it used to be called Respublika Sarayı or Republic Palace

Lighting in Baku metro station

nar Dagh, a mountain that's been on fire without interruption for more than a thousand years, thanks to the natural gas seeping from its surface.

'Pumpjacks of the World Unite!' could be the city's motto. Today, with oil prices hovering well above the legendary $100 per barrel mark, Baku is bustling again. The windfall has given the city a facelift, and, not to be outdone, the lumberjacks respond in kind as the city teems with construction sites for new buildings. If London and New York are turning green, Baku is still opting for the security, elegance, and stability that only black can offer.

Black, alas, doesn't go out of fashion, nor is this is an isolated or recent phenomenon: in the early twentieth century, Baku produced half the world's oil supply. Mansions were built by the likes of the Rothchilds and the Nobels, whose pissing contests consisted not only of whose house was larger, but, more importantly, whose tanker fleet was. (Answer: Nobel's.)

Today, the country's independence shapes the boom in both hard *and* soft ways. Where it once fuelled the Soviet Army against the Nazis, today it finances a cottage industry of content destined to flesh out a fragile Azerbaijani identity. An interesting exercise given that, before 1991, Azerbaijan as such never existed save for that short, twenty-three-month span just after the 1917 Bolshevik Revolution. What the West does with Helmut Newton or Muhammad Ali (produce coffee table books that compete with the size of the coffee table), Azerbaijan does with Heydar Aliyev (1923 – 2003), the former president and the current president's father.[1] An A2-sized hardback shows off full-bleed images of the Aliyevs at various functions, with the Clintons, or with Yasser Arafat. Another monumentally luxurious book with canvas box to boot is dedicated to Karabakh, a region officially belonging to Azerbaijan but occupied by Armenia since the early 1990s. The Azeris look to Karabakh much like the Serbs look to Kosovo: as a region with a particularly symbolic role in their national narrative.[2]

In the Icheri Sheher, or Old Town, a relatively well-preserved oasis from the concrete crunch of the city, I stumble across a real find: a facsimile re-issue of the entire series of *Molla Nasreddin*. Within the pages of this weekly rag, the young Azeri identity was being debated with no shortage of polemics – about language, sexism, religion – poking fun at the country's fragile position, club-sandwiched between Russia to the north and Iran to the south. The north's communism no longer threatens Azerbaijan though, and the Azeris seem rather immune to the creeping fundamentalism besetting its Caucasian neighbours. Pipeline politics seem

Dom Soviet (Government House), by M. Husseinov

Land of Lights by Tair Salakhov, 2005

Nobel oilwells 1890s, Baku, azer.com

to have cemented Baku's reputation: not only as the jewel of the Caspian but also as the Capital of Caucasian Cultural Exceptionalism. Wherever oil goes, so go I…

[1] The leader of Soviet Azerbaijan between 1969 and 1982, Heydar Aliyev succeeded to the presidency of independent Azerbaijan in 1993 and ruled the country for a decade with a firm hand. He was one of the driving forces behind the controversial BTC Baku-Ceyhan (Turkey) pipeline project, which bypasses both Russia and Iran.

[2] Yagub Mahmudov and Karim Shukurov, *Garabagh: Real History, Facts, Documents*, Tahsil Publishing House, Baku, 2005. Author's Note: this book clearly is a biased account of the contentious issue of Nagorno Karabagh, made by the Azerbaijanis.

Чвен ~~Сакартвелое~~
Сакуртвелос
Гаумарджос

By replacing the '*a*' with
a '*y*', TO OUR DEAR
GEORGIA becomes
TO OUR DEAR
KURDISTAN, and
presto, you've switched
the geopolitically
unresolved identity of
one mountain peoples
for another.

ჩვენ
საქართველოს
გაუმარჯოს!

To Mountain Minorities 2009, wall application

Changed Names

If ever there were a Slavs and Tatars religion, it would honour not people but names, with its only mortal sin being the Anglicisation of immigrants' or immigrants' children's names. A father went from Chengiz to Charles, a brother from Jacek to Jack, and a best friend from Naisohn to Steve. All have returned to their original names, Kazak, Polish, and Iranian, respectively. Too often the siren call of renaming traps not only those fresh off the boat, but also those fresh off the yacht, as any formerly rich Russian or Armenian could attest to. As other skies, alas, tell other stories, so do those emigrants who go east.

Teofil Łapiński / Theophile Lapinski / Taoufik Bey At the beginning of the nineteenth century, Poland ceased to exist on any map. Drafted into various countries fighting the Napoleonic wars, it was common to find Polish men and women ending up fighting each other, under the banners of France, Austria, or Russia.

Theophile Lapinski (1826 – 1886) was bathed in the rise of the Polish Liberation movement from a young age and was forced to flee Poland after the failed uprisings of 1848. He went on to participate in the Hungarian Revolution of 1848 – 49 as well as the Crimean War, on the side of the Europeans. But it was the Caucasus – with its romantic resistance against a much larger colossus, imperial Russia – which most captivated European revolutionary movements of the period. Lapinski decided to act on this affinity, by offering troops and artillery support.[1]

[1] Alexandre Grigoriantz, *Montagne du Sang*, Georg, Geneva,1998.

Boże, coś Polskę przez tak liczne wieki
Otaczał blaskiem potęgi i chwały,
Coś ją osłaniał tarczą swej opieki
Od nieszczęść, które pognębić ją miały.
ref.: Przed Twe ołtarze zanosim błaganie:

Ojczyznę wolną pobłogosław, Panie!

Ty, któryś potem tknięty jej upadkiem
Wspierał walczących za najświętszą sprawę,
I chcąc świat cały mieć jej męstwa świadkiem
W nieszczęściach samych pomnażał jej sławę.
ref.: Przed Twe ołtarze zanosim błaganie:

Ojczyznę wolną pobłogosław, Panie!

Wróć nowej Polsce świetność starożytną,
Użyźniaj pola, spustoszałe łany,
Niech szczęście, pokój, na nowo zakwitną,
Przestań nas karać, Boże zagniewany.
ref.: Przed Twe ołtarze zanosim błaganie:

Ojczyznę wolną pobłogosław, Panie!

Jedno Twe słowo, o wielki nasz Panie,
Zniszczyć i w prochy obrócić nas zdolne,
A gdy zasłużym na Twe ukaranie,
Obróć nas w prochy, ale w prochy wolne!
ref.: Przed Twe ołtarze zanosim błaganie:

Ojczyznę wolną pobłogosław, Panie!

Powstała z grobu na Twe władne słowo
Polska, wolności narodów chorąży,
Pierzchnęły straże, a ponad jej głową
Znowu swobodnie Orzeł Biały krąży!
ref.: Przed Twe ołtarze zanosim błaganie:

Ojczyznę wolną pobłogosław, Panie!

Boże, coś Polskę
(God Save Poland)
Hymn

[2] Lapinski went so far as to compare horticultural traditions of the Circassians with those of rural Europeans in Silesia, Poland and Hungary. See Aliy Berzegov, 'Teofil Lapinski: Hero and Leader of the Circassian War for Independence (Part One)', *North Caucasus Weekly,* Volume 9, Issue 22, June 2008.

In 1857 Lapinski, known under his *nom de guerre* Taoufik Bey, assembled a legion composed of between 6,000 and 15,000 Poles, and set to depart from Turkey to join the Circassians in the western Caucasus to battle the Russians. This force came to be known as one of the most formidable in the region, thanks in large part to Lapinski's methodical note-taking, which touched upon everything ranging from battle to harvesting methods of the Cherkess. A handful of the Poles forced to fight for Russia escaped their minders (two Russians to every Pole) and fled to the mountains where they would join forces with the mountain peoples under Lapinski's command. We imagine the Circassians singing in step with their Polish comrades, Boże, coś Polskę *(God Save Poland)* – never mind the difference in religion, skin colour, or intonation for that matter. The more deep-throated Turkic Circassian likely offered a much-needed aural ferocity to the softer Polish.[2]

David Urquhart / Daoud Pacha David Urquhart (1805 – 1877), whose intense Russophobia still causes us to hold our noses, called on the Circassians to unite and intensify an identity for a dispersed people stretching from the Black to the Caspian Sea. He went on to become Daoud Pacha, fighting on behalf of the Circassians in their struggle against the Ottomans and the Russians. In a review he founded called *The Portfolio*, which printed pieces about the Middle East and the Caucasus, he went so far as to publish the Circassian Declaration of Independence in 1836. Without a wink or a nod in sight, he penned a letter from London to his fellow Circassians on the date of 21 Reibul Akir 1251, or 1835. He wrote:

[3] David Urquhart, *The Portfolio. Collection of state papers illustrative of the history of our times,* James Ridgway and sons, London, Vol. I, no. IV and Vol. I, no. VII, 1836.

> *Let the Beys, the mollahs and the elders of the village call forth the people and read this letter and explain its contents. You will have the satisfaction to read the same words, from the Black Sea to the Caspian, and to hear yourself called by the same name, that of Circassians.*[3]

Circassians nmayd.com

David Urquhart / Daoud Pacha

Circassian Warrior during the Russian-Circassian War (1763 – 1864) circassianworld.com

Urquhart goes on to describe the solidarity that some 20,000 Poles, conscripts in the Russian army, will feel henceforth towards the Circassians. As will other peoples such as the Lezgis, Ossetians, Chechens, and Persians who all 'suffer from injustice and fear the aggression of their common enemy', revealing Urquhart's 'Great Game' grammar, in which the British and Russian empires are inevitably and irreparably pitted against one another. While he wasn't so successful in terms of realpolitik, Daoud Pacha hit a grand slam when it came to affection. The letter came accompanied with the first-ever design of the Circassian National Flag. This flag became known as the *sandjak cherif* [sacred standard], similar to the sacred standard of the prophet. It was treated with the same respect showed to Mohammed, even housed in a similar sanctuary at Soujouk Kala. To this day, however, the Circassians remain a forgotten nationality, even if they number over a million. Sadly, despite Daoud's own taste for it, it was again language that prevented them from successfully gaining recognition: the Circassians never managed to rally around a single, common language, the first step in forming a unified identity.

KEEP YOUR MAJORITIES CLOSE BUT YOUR MINORITIES CLOSER

Forever & Today
Grand Opening: 13 September 2008, 6-8 pm
141 Division Street, New York, NY 10002
info@foreverandtoday.org | www.foreverandtoday.org
Poster: Slavs and Tatars, 2008

Confluence of the Aragvi and Kura (Mtkvari) rivers, Mtskheta, Georgia wikipedia.org

Environments of Tiflis, down Kura river by De Kaprelevich, The New York Public Library *(left)*

Tbilisi: River Kura 1950s, The New York Public Library *(right)*

The Delicacy of Nano-Nationalism

Kumykistan or bust A nationalist and politician, Salau Aliyev is a case study in how one man's obscurities are another's national crisis. The founder of Tenglik ('Equality') in 1990, Aliyev is trying to claim autonomy for his fellow Kumyks, an ethnic people that was once the majority population in present-day Dagestan but now accounts for only fourteen per cent of its inhabitants.

Kabardiono–Balkaria Elbrus, circassianworld.com

Coat of arms of Dagestan

Salau Aliyev with Tenglik flag, from Karny, op cit.

In addition to speaking a Turkic language, the Kumyks practise a folk version of Sunni Islam, including pre-Islamic rituals. In *Highlanders: A Journey to the Caucasus in Quest of Memory*, Yoav Karny writes about Aliyev with equal measures of pity and affection, and talks of a man with a flag but without a state and delusions as to the Khazar origins of the Kumyks as 'a prehistoric motherland of great nations' where 'politicians do not strive to benefit only those who are living in the present, but also redeem cultures and nations long extinct.'[1] These very Khazars are believed to be the arbiters of Europe's salvation, responsible for keeping the Arab Umayyad forces at bay. In the eighth century, the Khazar royalty and aristocracy decided to convert en masse to Judaism, as a third way of triangulating between Byzantium's Christianity and the Caliphate's Islam.

[1] See Karny, op cit, p. 135.

Aliyev's attempt to go back more than a thousand years to settle a contemporary dispute is a vivid example of the collapse of time shared, not only across the Caucasus but across greater Eurasia:

[2] See also Kasia Korczak and Payam Sharifi, 'Slavs', *032c*, issue 11, 2006.

> *The vagaries of time are celebrated, ritualized, and collapsed. What happened four years ago is mentioned in the same breath, and what's more, with the same urgency as an event that transpired 400 years ago. So it follows that housing prices, interest rates, inflation and the like are as much a fault of Ivan the Terrible as Putin.*[2]

Slav + Turk > Slav + Persian Early-twentieth-century Eurasianists, including luminaries like linguist Roman Jakobson (1896 – 1982), often argued as to whether Slavs should look to the Turkic peoples (or Touran) or to the Persians in their search for cultural, linguistic, and political partners. The founder of Türé, a Balkar Nationalist Assembly, Bahauddin Etezov clearly sits in the former camp. All sorts of Touranians – especially the Young Turks – dream of uniting the Turkic peoples spread across an area stretching from Anatolia to Ulan Baator, and comprising not only Turkey, Azerbaijan, and parts of Russia's northern Caucasus, but also all Central Asian states, and some areas of Siberia, Bashkortostan and Mongolia.[3] Etezov himself believes in the very neat arithmetic of:

$$SLAV + TURK = RUSSIAN$$

A Balkarian, Etezov is primarily a dreamer. He has devoted his life to championing equal say for the significantly smaller region of Balkaria in the marriage of convenience uniting it with the more populous Kabardino in the Republic of Kabardino-Balkaria. This Caucasian region in Russia is one of the more stable ones in the area – especially when compared to Ossetia, Dagestan, or Ingushetia – although we imagine Etezov would be quite happy getting rid of that unwieldy hyphen and unleashing an eight republic on the small area separating the Black Sea in the west and the Caspian in the east. As much for his commitment as for his failure, we salute him.

Georgia (only) on my mind But those who strike out on their own fare no better, as the fate of fatalism's freelancers show. A writer-turned-diplomat-turned-opposition-turned émigré, Grigol Robakidze (1882 – 1962) was first and foremost a broken man. He led a life of continuous emotional disappointments in the Caucasus, with its fair share of sour surprises. A founder of the Georgian Union of Writers and fierce critic of Soviet policies, Robakidze had the very rare honour of having his play – *Lamara* (1928) – continue to be played in the USSR, even after his defection to Germany in 1930. When love of one's country becomes a glaucoma, it can only go downhill. He participated in right-wing Georgian organisations in Germany whose aim was to liberate Georgia from Soviet rule, including the Tetri Giorgi, accused of collaborating with the Germans during World War II. Today he lies in Leuville-sur-Orge, France, a burial ground known for its population of Georgian émigrés.

[3] Slavs and Tatars are critical of the excesses of pan-Turkism, responsible for the Turkish refusal to recognise non-Turkic minorities living within the Ottoman Empire or present-day Turkey. Concrete examples are the 1915 Armenian genocide or Turkey's refusal to recognise Kurds as a separate ethnic entity at the beginning of the twenty-first century, referring to them simply as Mountain Turks. See also 'Day XI' in *A Thirteenth Month Against Time*, 2008.

You can take the Slav out of Bulgaria, Poland, Slovenia, Slovakia, Russia, Serbia, Montenegro, Belarus, Croatia, Bosnia and Herzegovina, Macedonia, Ukraine, and the Czech Republic **but you can't take** Bulgaria, Poland, Slovenia, Slovakia, Russia, Serbia, Montenegro, Belarus, Croatia, Bosnia and Herzegovina, Macedonia, Ukraine, and the Czech Republic **out of the Slav.**

Slavs 2006, screenprint, 82 x 116 cm

WHEN YOU TRY

TWICE

Russian-Circassian War circassianworld.com

YOU LOSE

TWICE

On Pan-Caucasianism (or how the darkies tried to unite against the whiteys)

The highlanders of the Caucasus have attempted to bring different ethnic groups together several times by highlighting topographic proximity rather than divisive politics masquerading as ethnography. Our genuine respect for the advocacy of Pan-Caucasianism across the lines of the landscape is as varied as its results – whether we're speaking of those achieved by Imam Shamil, Yuri Shanibov or Mahmoud Ahmadinjed.

The village of Tindi Dagestan, late 1890s, by M. de Déchy, nationmaster.com

General Plievo statue Vladikavkaz, by Daniel J. Gerstle, 2006. He helped lead the Soviet Union defense against the Nazi German invasion in 1942. German forces were turned back just a few miles west of Vladikavkaz, North Ossetia

110-year old Talib Kardanov (Kabardian) is listening to his granddaughter playing national garmon. Kahun village, Urvanskij region, КБАССR, 1956, circassianworld.com

Once is never Yuri Magomedovich Shanibov's attempts to bring the mountain peoples together with the beautifully named but ineffectual Confederation of Mountain Peoples (1990), a militia of sixteen ethnic groups between Abkhazia and the North Caucases to Dagestan, was carnivalesque. A former professor of Marxism and Leninism and prosecutor, Shanibov tried to win independence for the North Caucasus before the dust of the Soviet break-up had settled, causing two, if not more, setbacks.

Shanibov (1936 –), a Caucasian, Circassian, Balkarian-Kabardino flip-flopper, has an elastic approach to ideology that has saved neither him nor his nation. He was arrested by the Russian Federal government, then let go of (according to him, he escaped), and even tried – in vain – to take back his leadership role of the Confederation, only to see himself further marginalised and ridiculed. But if in the West flip-flopping is soft and effete – one thinks of a crêpe – in the Caucasus it has all the delicacy of a pressure-cooker, causing pain either way.

Shanibov chose Russia's side in its support to Abkhazia during the war with Georgia in 1992 – 1993, then Chechnya's in its wars with Russia, only to throw in the sauna towel, drenched with discarded defeats, and tried to fault the U.S. for being behind it all along. The Americans, in his own words, 'have concluded that in the next century, the planet will be able to sustain only one billion people, and they are determined to make sure that all the survivors will be from the developed countries. I call them the "golden billion". The next global war will be fought not over oil but over clean air and fresh water. And the Caucasus being one of the ecologically cleanest areas in the world, will be reserved for the "golden billion" [...].'[1]

[1] See Karny, op cit, p 26.

A strange case of solidarity: Mahmoud Ahmadinejad As children, we are all taught to compare and contrast from an early age; at school, but for some also at home. The inner life of the immigrant child often differs drastically from his outer life. While young, these differences give us a sense of identity, of relevance. The indigenous child uses it to become a punk, goth, or hippy, while the immigrant uses difference to become, say, a straight-A student and skip a year in school.

If the child with a taste for what isn't right is endearing, excessive difference in adulthood makes for an eccentric at best, and an embittered old coot at worst. The émigré is a case in point here, essentially comparing and contrasting himself to irrelevance (see opposite page). And the more nations act like children, the more we're pushed to take on the airs of the elderly: calm, wise, and dedicated to drown the grating noise of contrast with the smooth jazz of comparison.

Today, there are tensions between the Russians and Caucasians, not to mention among the Caucasians themselves (between Azerbaijan, Georgia, and Armenia, as well as the southern Russian regions such as Dagestan, Chechnya and Ingushetia). But mention the name Ahmadinejad (1956 –) and it's a pretty picture of brotherhood among erstwhile enemies. Understandably, Azerbaijan and the majority-Muslim Russian Caucasus look to Ahmadinejad as a populist revolutionary demagogue, a president of a Modern Muslim theocracy, with a facile knack for sticking a thumb (the Iranian equivalent of the middle finger) in the face of the 'Great Satan', not to mention a certain weakness for revisionism.

But why would Georgia and Armenia, which are Christian, profess adulation for such a figure? These were among the first countries to adopt Christianity as a state religion. What's more: for Georgia, Christianity played a pivotal role in the development of its national consciousness and culture, especially given Persia's dominance at the time. Despite a common religion with the West, however, there remains a voluble, often overlooked anti-Western suspicion in these countries, which can only partially be explained as a vestige of communism. It might strike some as odd that Ahmadinejad, the polemical president of a Muslim theocracy, appeals to the remnants of a left-leaning and largely atheist ideology but it speaks volumes about the role radical Islam plays today in filling the space left by the failure of these very movements. While the West looks to Ahmadinjed as a source of instability in the region, the Near, Middle, and somewhat Far East look to him as a source of anti-imperialist solidarity.

"RUSSIA: WE KNOW IT. THEY DON'T. BUT THEY'LL FIND OUT."[1]

II/32

History hasn't been kind to Alexander Herzen. He has been doubly condemned. Force-fed to every Russian school-child during Communism, Herzen suffers from an unjustified, if understandable, resistance to his work within his home country. Outside Russia, the situation is not much better: he has been almost entirely eclipsed by his contemporary–Marx–whose categorical and highly structural thought has been more *actionable* than Herzen's preference for subtlety, sophistication, and contradiction. If you've got an MBA, Marx is your man. PhD holders, turn to Herzen.

Few things are more attractive than a person who is *of his time*, who lives thoroughly his epoch, who is commensurate with it. It is one thing to live such a life, and a rarer thing still to document it. Herzen did both and his *My Past and Thoughts*, an 8-volume autobiography, has become a quiet benchmark of the art of recollection. The differing scale of tragedy–whether his son's premature death or the failure of the 1848 revolutions–is not approached with pincers or shelved but explored intimately, with a sense of urgency in his very language. There are few sound bytes but much to chew on.

While American universities still struggle to differentiate between Marxist, Marxian and Marxesque, we turn to Herzen's humanism and swim in its complexity, hoping one day we can all be Herzian.

1. Stoppard, Tom. "The Coast of Utopia: Shipwreck" (New York: Grove Press, 2002)

Desperate, Djadid, or dandy? Before Ahmadinejad, another figure inspired a similar sense of Pan-Caucasianism, one that had nothing to do with early-twenty-first-century anti-Americanism, but rather a nineteenth-century tide of anti-Russian sentiment. Imam Shamil (1797 – 1871) led various campaigns of guerrilla-warfare against the Russians during the Caucasian War (1817 – 1864) and was known for being able to unite the famously warring tribes of the region.

Shamil, Imam of Chechnya and Dagestan by P. A. Glushkov, (Lithographer), 1870, New York Public Library

Shamyl wikipedia.org

Surrender of Shamil by Franz Roubaud, varvar.ru

Marx called him 'a desperate democrat' but there was clearly more than just politics to his life. After twenty years of guerrilla-resistance and improbable escapes, one morning Shamil woke up with the realisation that compromise need not mean surrender. After a brief stint in a prison outside Moscow, where he complained of the cold temperatures, he took up residence in a posh villa in Kiev in what was then very much part of the Russian empire. Tsar Alexander III footed the bill and Shamil wrote, incredibly, that he was quite grateful (to Allah, of course, not Alexander) for his current situation: the climate was pleasant and the surrounding mountains reminded him of his home.

The mountain people are a tough people indeed. But cultural convenience has us forget that toughness begets an acute appreciation for luxury: Caucasians are also an eminently epicurean lot. Clearly, Shamil was no exception, with a sartorial taste for the outfits he wore on walks in the Tsar's garden. Dressed in bear fur, yellow Moroccan boots, and a white turban (the latter with special permission from the Tsar), the Lion of Dagestan cut a striking silhouette.

Circassian woman from James Hunter's *Young People's History of the World,* The International Publishing Company, Philadelphia, 1897

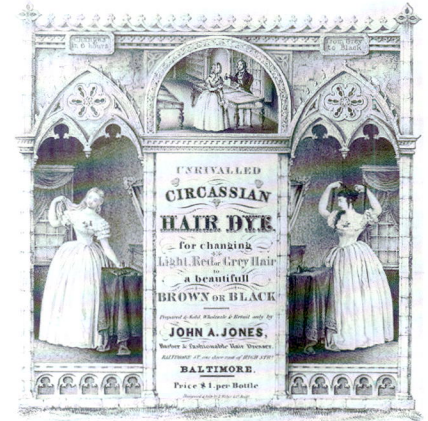

A poster from c.1843 advertising Circassian Hair Dye 'for changing light, red or grey hair to a beautiful brown or black'

Circassian Beauty The women of the Circassian people of the North Caucasus were idealised beginning in the eighteenth century for their reputed beauty, spirit and elegance. They occupied Sultans' Harems during the Ottoman Empire, and later became characterised as the ideal of feminine beauty in poetry, novels, art – and advertising, the name 'Circassian' becoming commonly used in naming beauty products claiming to be used by the women of Circassia. In the late-nineteenth century, showmen such as P.T. Barnum, too, began to capitalise on this reputation, exhibiting women he claimed to be of Circassian origin in his sideshow attractions. Portrayed as refined and genteel women who had escaped a life of sexual slavery, Barnum's Circassian beauties wore a distinctive tall, teased hairstyle, not unlike the Afros of the 1970s.
Images: wikipedia.org

The Harem – Introduction of an Abyssinian slave by John Frederick Lewis, 1860

It is a curse to be wished upon no one: one of your countries invades the other. If in war there are no winners, only losers, then when both sides belong to you, you lose exponentially. Or, to paraphrase Winston Churchill on Russia, it is somewhat like suffocation wrapped in anxiety, buried deep inside frustration.

I bookended the summer of 2008 with a trip to Tbilisi in May and a conversation with Nina Gomiashvili, founder of Moscow's Pobeda Gallery, in September, to discuss the collision of the political and the personal as a result of the five-day war in August between Georgia and Russia. Nina is the daughter of one of the USSR's most accomplished actors, a Georgian by the name of Arshil Gomiashvili, and a Russian, and a mother herself. I figured that her dual identity – shared between erstwhile friends and now outright enemies – would at the very least serve as an antidote to an eventual conflict between the U.S. and Iran.

THE POLITICAL

Despite my use of earplugs at night, I have grown accustomed to the drum beat of war from one of my countries, the U.S., towards the other, Iran. Georgia's relationship with Russia, however, is a far more intimate, delicate, and layered affair than the pre-teen name-calling that passes for diplomacy between the 'Great Satan' and the 'Rogue Nation' I call homes. Traditionally sandwiched between the Turks, the Persians, and the Russians, the

Aleksander Griboyedov Left Embankment

Orthodox Priest

Memorial to the victims of April 9, 1989 Rusthaveli Avenue

Georgians, politically and religiously, often sided with Russia, going so far as to voluntarily relinquish sovereignty in the early nineteenth century in exchange for protection from incessant Persian attacks. As complexity is often the first casualty of war, Nina recounted the story of the first flare-up between Russia and Georgia in 2006:

Actually the thing I fear the most is that people here have a very general, vague impression of what's going on there and vice versa. A couple of years ago, when there was the diplomatic conflict between Russia and Georgia, the police came to my daughter's school and asked the Dean for a list of the kids with Georgian last names. Well, thankfully, the Dean said 'fuck off'. He's got steel balls.

What did they want?

They wanted to know where Georgian families are registered, where they lived, what they were doing. And where do you go? You don't go around the homes or offices. You go to schools. Especially private schools, where the children of the Georgian elite can afford to go.

THE PERSONAL

I intended to travel to Tbilisi to deliver an intimate, if somewhat late, Iranian-American apology for a resolutely Persian crime. My early-nineteenth-century Persian forefathers had mobbed the Russian embassy and killed

Alexander Griboyedov (1795 – 1829), who penned the play whose words are so robust that they travel business-class from the original Russian to the scrappier shores of the English economy: Горе от ума, or *Woe from Wit*.[1]

Six months prior to his death, Griboyedov had married a sixteen-year-old Georgian princess by the name of Nino Chauchavadze. When she learnd of his death, the pregnant Nino was devastated, resulting in a stillbirth. She remained a widow until her death forty years later and has since become a legend of romantic devotion – in a region which rates romance more than highly. Nino returned the favour of Griboyedov's eloquence, posthumously, by writing on his tombstone:

УМЪ И ДѢЛА ТВОИ БЕЗ
СМЕРТНЫ ВЪ ПАМЯТИ
РУССКОЙ, НО ДЛЯ ЧЕГО
ПЕРЕЖИЛА ТЕБЯ ЛЮБОВЬ
МОЯ!

Your intelligence and work are eternal in Russian memory
But why did my love have to out-live you!

Nino's inscription reminded me of Nina's warning: 'You know, these mountain people, their memories are just fine. With Georgians, Ossetians, etc., you know entire generations will be fucked up. It's in their blood. You kill my neighbour, I kill you and your entire family. It may be from the sixteenth century, but it still exists. And that's the worst thing.'

Ministry of Highways of the Georgian Soviet Socialist Republic, by G. Chakhava and Z. Dzhalaganya, 1977

State Museum of Anthropology and Ethnography

Laguna Vera pool

Memory, it seems, is not in short supply in this area of the world, and might be one trait best not shared among erstwhile friends and now enemies.

[1] Aleksander Griboyedov was a Russian playwright and diplomat to the Caucasus and Persia. A promising young literary talent and friend of Pushkin, Griboyedov died prematurely during a trip to enforce the Treaty of Turkmenchay when a Persian mob attacked the Russian embassy in Tehran. See Laurence Kelly, *Diplomacy and Murder in Tehran*. TPP, London, 2006.

IT IS
OF UTMOST
IMPORTANCE
THAT
WE REPEAT
OUR MISTAKES
AS A REMINDER
TO FUTURE
GENERATIONS
OF THE DEPTHS
OF OUR STUPIDITY

One of the *Wrong and Strong* series, 2005, offset print, 42 x 59.4 cm (each)

When You Try Thrice, You Lose Thrice

The wise fool and the alphabet that fools around It was via a complete re-edition of *Molla Nasreddin* that we fell in love with the devastating tides of changes to the Azeri alphabet. Before one can translate one must first know how to decipher. With at least three changes to the alphabet – from Arabic to Latin to Cyrillic to Latin – within 100 years, the Azeri script presented its own set of hurdles. Before we could even begin to think about *what*, we needed to know *how*. It's one thing to find a translator for a language spoken by four million people, but another thing entirely for that translator to also know the two previous iterations of their own language.

Illustrations from *Molla Nasreddin* vol I-II, 1906-09, Azerbaijan Dovlet Nasriyyati and vol III, 1909-1910, Çinar-Çap, Baku. Each volume of the 10-piece set is re-issued with 2 to 3 year intervals

But our problems pale in comparison to the tragic loss such ruptures in linguistic continuity cause for generations of Azeris, past, present and future. The changes in the alphabet essentially made Azeris immigrants in their own country – immigrants vis-à-vis other generations: grandparents couldn't read the language their grandchildren were taught at school. And immigrants vis-à-vis their own cultural legacy: for example, books in Arabic were destroyed, resulting in the disappearance of many texts, but of particular note was an important body of work in Islamic natural medicine.

Molla Nasreddin was an Azeri political satire, edited by Jalil Mammadguluzadeh, printed in the Caucasus between 1906 and 1930. The itinerant nature of the periodical's offices – first located in Tbilisi (now Georgia, then Russian Empire), then Tabriz (Iran), and finally Baku (now Azerbaijan) – capture the region's upheaval during this particular period best. *Molla Nasreddin* was a polemical journal: advocating women's rights, pressing for the latinisation of the alphabet, and poking fun at colonial threats, whether it was socialism from Russia to the north or Islamicisation from Iran to the south. The publication contributed greatly to an understanding of self-identity for a fledgling republic – of Azerbaijan – that would briefly exist for two years just after the 1917 Bolshevik Revolution, only to disappear within the Soviet Union until 1991.

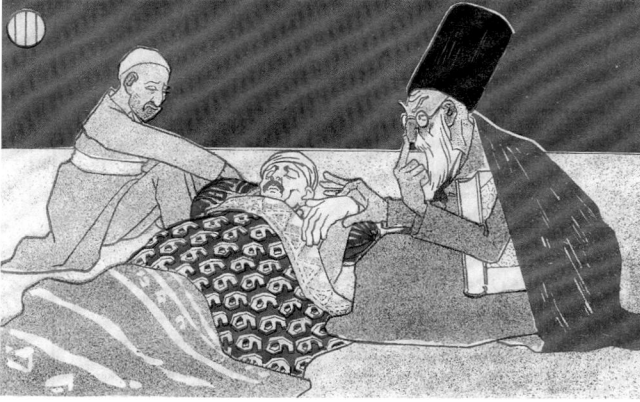

The weekly journal was renowned for its illustrations – biting caricatures on its covers or double-page spreads that took issue with such diverse matters as Ottoman meddling, Russian bureaucracy and Iranian proselytising, never missing a chance to poke fun at local collusion with foreign powers and their colonial ambitions. The periodical was named after a twelfth-century legendary folkloric character found throughout the region, from Bulgaria all the way to China. Nasreddin's own humour is as misleadingly simple as the journal named after him – it's neither ironic nor distant. Instead, the one-liner or slapstick 'ha-ha-ha' reveals a political, philosophical, or, at times, moral critique. It's a generous, rubbery, elastic wisdom, allowing for contradiction, sometimes both irrational and rational, smart and dumb.

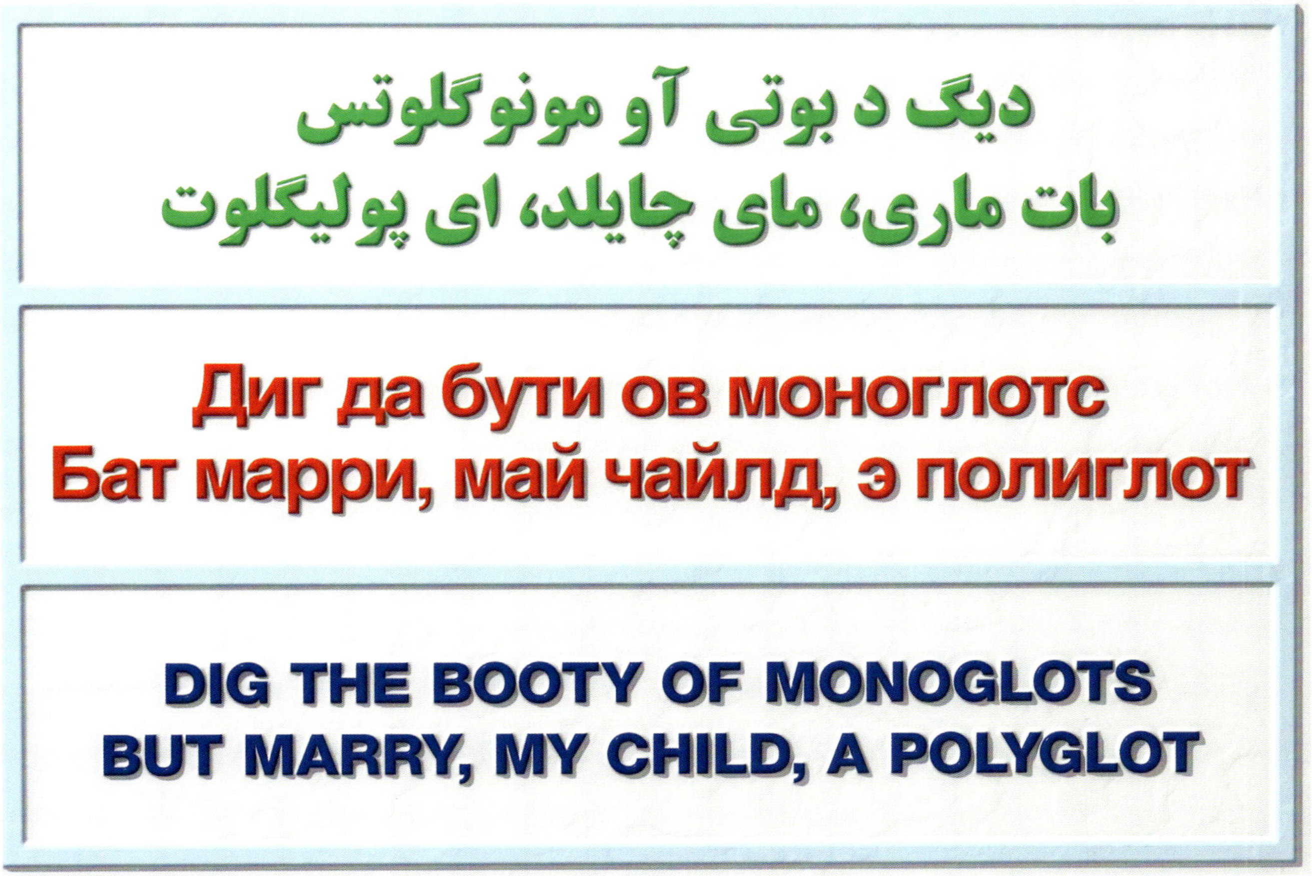

Dig the Booty 2009, vacuum-formed plastic, 100 x 70 cm

FOOL ME ONCE,

SHAME ON ARABIC.

FOOL ME TWICE,

SHAME ON CYRILLIC.

FOOL ME THRICE,

SHAME ON LATIN:

AaaaaaaahhhhhZERI!!!

THE STORY OF THE ALPHABET THAT COULD NOT DECIDE

AaaaaaahhhhZERI!!!
2009, screenprint,
70 x 100 cm

Alphabet in the Boiling Pot of Politics

Conservatively speaking, the Azerbaijani or Azeri alphabet to date has been altered four times--to Arabic after the Islamic conquest; to Latin (1928-1938); to Cyrillic (1939-1991) and to Latin again (1991 to present). On each occasion, the motivation for change was political. However, if we consider the replacement of a single letter in any of the phonetic alphabets (Cyrillic or Latin), then the Azeri alphabet has been changed at least ten times (Tables 2,3,4). Nor does this take into account the pre-Islamic scripts used by the Turkic nations and other ancestors of modern Azerbaijanis such as Caucasian Albanians. If those are added, then the historical figure would be raised to twelve or more, depending on how far back one digs in search of ancient scripts. (See next page bottom Table).

ISLAM-the First Political Reason for Changing the Alphabet

For many centuries after the conquest of Islam, the only official written language in the conquered lands, including Azerbaijan, was Arabic as the Islamic caliphate had to create a lingua franca to unify their territory. When these nations began using their own languages for reading and writing, the Arabic alphabet was retained. The most valuable contribution that the Arabic alphabet made for the Turkic tribes and nations was to provide them with a more-or-less universal script (the Arabic letters generally do not express all the vowel sounds which is one of the most obvious differences between various dialects and closely-related Turkic languages). Hence, this common means of communication made the great poet and philosopher Fizuli as much Turkish (Ottoman) as he was Azerbaijani or the great thinker of Turkistan, Ali-Shir Navayi, as much understood in Tabriz as in Bukhara.

On the other hand, since the Middle Ages, it is precisely because the Arabic script does not express the vowels that it was so strongly criticized.[1] However, it wasn't until the 20th century that the Arabic alphabet was totally replaced by another script.

The first attempts to alter the Arabic script (1860-1870) were made by three individuals: Manif Pasha, a scholar in the Turkish court; Malkom Khan, an Iranian Armenian intellectual in the Russian Embassy in Tehran; and Akhunzadeh, the great Azerbaijani thinker, writer, and dramatist, who was the most active of all. All three were friends who wanted to westernize Muslim society. Akhundzadeh, an atheist, pushed for the reform to counter Islamic culture though none could ever have dared to suggest adoption of the Latin alphabet as it would have been blasphemous.[2] Instead, they pushed to eliminate the dots, express each vowel and make the writing smoother and more continuous. Akhundzadeh believed that one of the main reasons for "backwardness" among the Muslim world laid in their style of education which was based on the Arabic alphabet. As their reformist proposals were considered political and anti-Islamic both by Istanbul and Tehran, they were rejected.[3]

Soviet Rule Bans the Arabic Alphabet

After the death of Akhundzadeh in 1878, the issue of "modernizing the alphabet" was forgotten for a while, at least in official circles. After the Revolution of 1917 and the fall of the Tsarist Empire, Azerbaijanis established their own independent Republic which survived from 1918 until 1920 during which time the

[1] Abu Reyhan Biruni has emphasized the necessity of using "E'rab" signs for vowels) in the Arabic script in his book, Al sidle--on Seeds and Fruits--in Arabic.

[2] Algar, Hamid. Malkum Khan, Akhundzadeh and the Proposed Reform of the Arabic Alphabet, Middle Eastern Studies. 5, 1969.

[3] Algar Hamid. 1969. Religions and State in Iran, 1785-1906: The Qajar Period. Berkeley and Los Angeles.

CHANGES IN AZERBAIJANI ALPHABET WITHIN 20TH CENTURY

Modified Arabic after Islam*	Old Latin 1929-1939*	Cyrillic 1939-1991* (earlier types)	New Latin 1991-date (earlier types)	Examples in new Latin (translations)
	A - a	A - a	A - a	Ana (mother)
	B - b	Б - б	B - b	Baş (head)
	C - c	Ч - ч	C - c	Can (soul)
	Ç - ç	Ч - ч	Ç - ç	Çay (tea)
	D - d	Д - д	D - d	Daş (stone)
	E - e	E - e	E - e	Ev (house)
	Ə - ə	Ə - ə	Ə - a (Ä-a)	əl (hand)
	F - f	Ф - ф	F - f	Fil (elephant)
	G - g	К - к	G - g	Göz (eye)
	Ğ - ğ	Ғ - ғ	Ğ - ğ	bağ (garden)
	H - h	h - h	H - h	Hara (where)
	X - x	X - x	X - x	Xaç (cross)
	I - i	И - и	i - i	İlan (snake)
	ь - ь	ы - ы (ь - ы)	I - ı	İldırım (thunder)
	Z - z	Ж - ж	J - j	Jalə (dew)
	K - k	К - к	K - k	Kim (who)
	L - l	Л - л	L - l	Lalə (tulip)
	M - m	М - м	M - m	Maral (deer)
	N - n	Н - н	N - n	Nar (pomegranate)
	O - o	O - o	O - o	Ora (there)
	Ö - ö	Ө - ө	Ö - ö	Özgə (other)
	P - p	П - п	P - p	Pay (share)
	Q - q	Г - г	Q - q	Qar (snow)
	R - r	Р - р	R - r	Rəqs (dance)
	S - s	С - с	S - s	Sən (you)
	Ş - ş	Ш - ш	Ş - ş	Şən (cheerful)
	T - t	Т - т	T - t	Tanrı (god)
	U - u	У - у	U - u	Uca (tall)
	Y - y	Y - y	Ü - ü	Ürək (heart)
	V - v	В - в	V - v	Varlıq (existence)
	J - j	J - j (Я-я)	Y - y	Yay (summer)
	Z - z	З - з	Z - z	Zirvə (peak)
	'	'		' (apostrof) Ma'lum (known)

* Modified Arabic script is still in popular use in Southern (Iranian) Azerbaijan.
* Conversion to Latin was proposed in 1922, but it was not officially established till 1929.
* Latin Alphabet continued to be in use till mid-40s and after adaptation of Cyrillic.

Sample 1: AN ANCIENT TURKIC LITHOGRAPH

__Monument of "Kültigin"; in Orkhon-Yenisey script*; 7-11th century AD__

Source: "VARLIQ" No.83-04/1992; Tehran, p.9

*The monument of "Kültigin" devoted to the famous Turkic ruler, Prince Kültigin (685-731 AD), is one of the Orkhon-Yenisey scripts which were found near the Orkhon river in Mongolia. Orkhon-Yenisey alphabet were used by the Turkic nations before they accepted Islam.

government continued publishing all its official correspondence in the Arabic alphabet and the issue of Latinization was officially never raised.

In 1920, the Bolsheviks toppled the Democratic Republic of Azerbaijan. It was the "Soviet of Azerbaijan People's Commissars," set up by the Communists which in late 1921 organized the "New Alphabet Committee." This was before any change had taken place in Turkey regarding alphabet reform.

In 1926 the first Turkology Conference was held in Baku which provided the linguistic and scientific justification for the Latin script which was adopted finally in 1929 ("Old Latin"-Table 2). For the Soviets, Latinizing the alphabet was a means of severing the Muslim population from their past and of preventing outside influence. This process was not confined to Azerbaijan but was carried out throughout the entire Turkic Muslim population of the Soviet Union. In 1928, the Republic of Turkey replaced the traditional Arabic alphabet with Latin. Although their motivations were similar to the Soviets--centralization, westernization and disassociation with the Islamic past--the modifications to the script were significant enough to make reading between the Latin scripts of the Soviet Republics and Turkey difficult. Whether this was intentional is not clear.

Stalin Rules Out Latin

Although Lenin had called Latinization "the great revolution of the east," in 1939 the official *Literaturnaya Gazeta* disagreed and wrote "the Latin script does not provide all the necessary conditions for bringing the other people (nationalities) closer to the great Russian people's culture." Overnight, the Turkic populations of Soviet Union were forced to convert to a new alphabet--Cyrillic. This decision was so sudden that in Azerbaijan alone, certain characters were changed several times (Table 4).

Conversion to Cyrillic was carried out with two main goals: Russification and isolation between Turkic nations. The second goal was achieved by using different Cyrillic characters for the same sounds in various Turkic languages; for example, the symbol "o" was used in Uzbek for the same sound that appeared as an "a" in Azeri, etc. The variety was sufficiently complex so that ordinary people of each nationality were not able to communicate in writing with each other.

An illustration of the evidence of alphabet changes in Azerbaijan even on grave markers -- here in Arabic and Cyrillic. (Sufi Hamid Cemetery, one hour south of Baku). Photo: Farid Mamedov

With Glasnost came Alphabetical Perestroika[4]

In 1985 with Gorbachev's nomination as the new leader of the Soviet Union, the new policy of Glasnost was announced. The first signs of this new political openness in Azerbaijan became evident by the enormous number of articles in Azeri newspapers criticizing the colonialist nature of the Cyrillic alphabet and the need to revive the old alphabet (Arabic). This movement was led by the famous poet and writer, Bakhtiyar Vahabzade, who in his long dramatic poem, "Iki Qorkhu" (Two Fears) describes how Stalin first used the Latin and then the Cyrillic alphabet to separate Azerbaijan from its thousand year old literature and southern brothers and sisters. Other pro-traditional alphabet articles followed.[5] Ziya Buniadov, a famous Azerbaijani scholar, was the first to call for a return to the Latin alphabet in July 1989.[6] The issue soon divided Azerbaijani intellectuals into pro-Latinists and pro-Arabists. Heated discussions extended beyond geographical boundaries into Iran and Turkey and took on a political entity of their own. The days of Glasnost were over and the days of the "Great Game"[7] made the alphabet yet again a victim of political competition and purges.

The "Great Game" and the Azeri Alphabet

The alphabet was the main ingredient in the boiling pot of Turkish-Iranian politics. While the Latin alphabet came to symbolize a propensity for the West, secularism, and pro-

Turkism; the Arabic (Koranic) alphabet was clearly associated with the Islamic Republic of Iran and all its religious ramifications. Each competitor used different tactics to promote their own script. Iran began increasing the number of publications available to their own Azerbaijani populations. (Publication in Azeri had been forbidden in Iran during the Pahlavi era from 1925-79) except during the brief period from 1941 to 1946 when the country was occupied by Allied forces.[8]

Many Azeri publications of the Revolution (1979-81) did not survive under Islamic rule. In 1989, there was only one single Azeri publication, Varliq, produced quarterly, half in Persian, half in Azeri from the private resources of Dr. Javad Heyat. Varliq only had a circulation of 2,000 despite the fact that more than 20 million Azerbaijanis lived in Iran. However the Iranian government suddenly started devoting pages for Azeri in its official papers; even the publication of Azeri books was somehow encouraged.[9] Often these papers concerned Northern Azerbaijanis more than Iranian Azerbaijanis. A typical article would promote the Arabic alphabet reminding the reader that the revival of Islam in Azerbaijan demanded the revival of the Arabic alphabet.[10] The most convincing and scientific of these articles, however, was published in Varliq by Dr. Abbas-Ali Javadi in 1369-1370 (1992).

In any case, northern Azerbaijani intellectuals argued that they did not have a

---

[4] Glasnost--"political openness" and Peristroika--"restructuring" were two terms introduced by Gorbachev and which soon became part of the international vocabulary. In Azeri, they were called ashkarliq and yeniden qurma.

[5] Abbas-Ali Javadi. 1990. Alphabet Changes. Varliq. Winter (1369, pp. 24-29; Summer (1370) pp. 88-96; Autumns (1370) pp. 91-102.

[6] Audrey L. Alstadt. 1992. The Azerbaijani Turks: Power and

Identity under the Russian Rule. Hoover Institution Press. Stanford University, Stanford, CA, p. 209.

[7] The "Great Game" was a term used to refer to the political competition in the Middle East between Russian and Britain during the 19th century. Recently many journalists have used it to refer to the competition between Iran and Turkey over the former Soviet republics.

[8] Yarshater, Ehsan, Ed., 1992 Encyclopaedia Iranica. Javadi, H. and

K. Burrill in "Azeri Literature in Iran." Routledge & Kegan Paul: London. p. 251.

[9] Official papers like Kayhane Havayi and Etela'at printed a few pages of Azeri in the Arabic alphabet. In Tabriz the new Azeri papers like Sahand and Ark have been published and Islami Birlik even includes a few pages in the Cyrillic alphabet.

[10] There are more or less similar articles on this topic in almost every issue of the journal, Yol, between 1990-1992.

role model for the Arabic alphabet as Iranian Azerbaijan did not provide them with a strong literary basis for revival of the Arabic alphabet. The monthly *Odlar Yurdu* published in Baku went so far as to argue that if the Iranian government established Azerbajani schools where Azeri would be taught in Arabic alphabet, then the North would welcome this by adopting the Arabic alphabet instead of Latin. In itself, this was a very political argument. It was like saying, "You have no right to tell us what to do when your own Azeris don't even have a single school in their own mother tongue."

This, along with various other reasons, including the lack of expertise with the Arabic alphabet and its more tedious spelling and writing techniques made the Turkish position for the Latin script stronger. Turkey busily organized many linguistic seminars and conferences on the Turkic alphabet. The most well known conference, "The Common Alphabet of the Turkic Nations," was held in Ankara in October of 1990 and organized by the Turkish Language History Organization (Türkiye Dil Tarik Kurumu). In many of these seminars and conferences, the arguments set forth were extremely political: "A common alphabet is essential for bringing together all the Turks of the world." In other words, that which the Arabic alphabet had already done for many centuries was now expected from Latin. The phonetic nature of Latin made it too difficult to hide the differences between them as had been done with Arabic. This created another question of what would happen to all the sounds which existed in the Turkic languages other than those that existed in the Turkish language? The radical answer was "get rid of them, make them sound just like Turkish."

As one of the participants of the First International Congress of Azerbaijan Turkish Associations (Istanbul, November 1990), I was surprised that one of the leaders of the Motherland (Anaveten) party gave a "speech" basically declaring, "Your alphabet must be exactly the same as ours." That a major Turkish party leader was asking Azerbaijanis to copy the Turkish Latin made the issue of alphabet so political it was hard to believe that there was any other motivation behind it.

It could be argued that Turkey won the "Great Game" of the alphabet. In May of 1990, the Republic Supreme Soviet of Azerbaijan established a commission to work on the Latinization 20 and on December 25, 1991, the National Council of the Republic of Azerbaijan officially replaced the Cyrillic script with a modified Latin alphabet (See table 2)

But the Latin alphabet which the Azerbaijanis adopted was not identical to the Turkish script. The new Azeri Latin now has three letters which do not exist in Turkish Latin - x (kh sound), upside down "e" (ae sound in "fat cat") and q, which express sounds particular to the Azeri language which do not exist in Turkish. Initially, a two-dotted (ä) was designed for expressing the vowel sound in the English word, "and". The idea was to make it look as similar to Turkish and European alphabet as possible as well as to be able to use foreign typewriters and ready-made software. It must also be mentioned that one of the criticisms against using the Arabic script was its cumbersome use of dots which made writing so tedious. But, because this sound is so frequent in Azeri, and the dots so cumbersome, six months later, they reverted to the up-side down "e" - a symbol that had become very familiar to their eye as it had been used both in the early Latin alphabet in 1928 and had even survived Cyrillization.

Conclusion

Changing the alphabet so many times in Azerbaijan has had severe consequences on the accumulative wealth of knowledge and culture of the nation. It has hindered continuity of the literary development, isolating the people from centuries of knowledge, cultural insight and human wisdom. It has erected intellectual barriers between generations. Children often can't read their parents' writing much less that of their grandparents. And in some cases, brothers and sisters have even experienced this separation and isolation from one another.

Alphabet change has created an incredible financial strain on the society. Who pays for all the street signs and government documents that must be transliterated much less the thousands of books which should be re-published?

At different times in its history, alphabet changes have served to isolate Northern Azerbaijan from Southern Azerbaijan. If the Araz river was the "natural" border between the two Azerbaijanis and if the barbed wires emphasized physical separation; then alphabet differences created a third boundary -- an invisible cultural one.

It has served to isolate Azerbaijan from related Turkic-speaking peoples and from the West. But, perhaps, the greatest tragedy to what is nearly a century old process is that if alphabet change is carried out solely, or even, partially, for political purposes, the damage can be catastrophic, as future purges by the ruling politics will again and again make the "defenseless" alphabet--its victim.

by Abulfazl Bahadori

We Are Our Mountains (Մենք ենք մեր սարերը) by S. Paghtassarian, Stepanakert. Also known as *Tatik and Papik* (Տատիկ եւ Պապիկ) in eastern Armenian and *Mamig yev Babig* (Մամիկ եւ Պապիկ) in western Armenian. It is a large monument from tufa of an old Armenian man and woman hewn from rock, representing the mountain people of Karabagh.

Front page of the *Komunist of Sumgait* newspaper (no.26, 1988), M. S. Gorbachev's appeal to people of Azerbaijan and Armenia (in view of the tragic events in Nagorno-Karabagh) *(left)*

Image taken during the tragic events in Nagorno-Karabagh from *Two year tragedy: Photochronicles and events* by A. Sharifov and others, Azerneshr Publishing, Baku, 1990 *(right)*

ПРОЛЕТАРИИ ВСЕХ СТРАН, СОЕДИНЯЙТЕСЬ!

КОММУНИСТ СУМГАИТА

Газета выходит с 1952 года

ОРГАН СУМГАИТСКОГО ГК КП АЗЕРБАЙДЖАНА И ГОРСОВЕТА НАРОДНЫХ ДЕПУТАТОВ

28 ФЕВРАЛЯ 1988 года ВОСКРЕСЕНЬЕ № 26 (5572)

АЗӘРБАЈҸАН КП СУМГАЈЫТ ШӘҺӘР КОМИТӘСИНИН ВӘ ШӘҺӘР ХАЛГ ДЕПУТАТЛАРЫ СОВЕТИНИН ОРГАНЫ

Цена 3 коп.

Обращение Генерального секретаря ЦК КПСС М. С. ГОРБАЧЕВА к трудящимся, к народам Азербайджана и Армении

Дорогие товарищи!

Обращаюсь к вам в связи с событиями в Нагорном Карабахе и вокруг него.

Поднят вопрос о переходе этой автономной области из Азербайджанской ССР в состав Армянской ССР. Этому придали остроту и драматичность, которые привели к напряженности и даже к действиям, выходящим за рамки закона.

Скажу откровенно: ЦК КПСС обеспокоен таким развитием событий, они чреваты самыми серьезными последствиями.

Мы не за то, чтобы уклоняться от откровенного обсуждения различных идей и предложений. Но делать это надо спокойно, в рамках демократического процесса и законности, не допуская ни малейшего ущерба интернациональной сплоченности наших народов. Нельзя отдавать серьезнейшие вопросы народной судьбы во власть стихии и эмоций.

Очень важно — оценить свои заботы в контексте не только местных условий, но и с учетом развернувшихся в стране процессов революционного обновления.

Да, в нашей жизни есть нерешенные проблемы. Но разногласия от распрей и недоверия народов друг к другу только помешают их решению. Это шло бы вразрез с нашими социалистическими принципами и нашей нравственностью, с традициями дружбы и братства советских людей.

Мы живем в многонациональной стране, более того — все республики, многие области, да и города и поселки у нас — многонациональны. И смысл ленинской национальной политики состоит в том, чтобы каждый человек, каждая нация могли свободно развиваться, чтобы важнейший народ мог удовлетворять свои потребности во всех сферах общественно-политической жизни, в родном языке и культуре, в обычаях и верованиях.

Социалистический интернационализм — источник огромной нашей силы. Подлинное братство и единение народов — вот наш путь.

Хорошо сказал великий армянский поэт Е. Чаренц, обращаясь к Советскому Азербайджану: «Во имя прошлого безмерного страдания, во имя жизни, нам представшей средь побед, во имя дружного союза, созидания, — народу братскому мы шлем привет, привет».

И как перекликаются с этими словами великого сына азербайджанского народа С. Вургуна: «Мы живем не по соседству, а в

друг в друге. Народы издавна брали друг у друга огонь для очага и хлеб насущный.

Ни одна мать не согласится с тем, чтобы ее детям угрожали национальные распри взамен прочных уз дружбы, равенства, взаимопомощи — поистине великого обретения социализма.

В Нагорно-Карабахской автономной области накопилось немало недостатков и трудностей. Новое руководство области должно принять срочные меры для исправления положения. Центральный Комитет КПСС дал на этот счет четыре рекомендации и будет непосредственно следить за их выполнением.

Сейчас самое главное — сосредоточиться на преодолении сложившейся ситуации, на решении накопившихся экономических, социальных, экологических и других проблем, накопившихся в Азербайджане и Армении, в духе развития перестройки и обновления, осуществляемой во всей нашей стране.

Надо дорожить и всемерно укреплять традиции дружбы между азербайджанским и армянским народами, сложившиеся за годы Советской власти. Только такой подход отвечает подлинным интересам всех народов СССР.

Вы знаете, что есть намерение специально посвятить раз-

витию национальных отношений Пленум Центрального Комитета нашей партии. Предстоит обсудить широкий круг вопросов этой важнейшей общественной сферы и на базе принципиальных завоеваний ленинской национальной политики наметить пути конкретного решения социально-экономических, культурных, и других проблем.

Все мы с вами — советские граждане. У нас общая история, общие победы, за плечами великий труд, горести и утраты. Мы заняты великим делом перестройки, от успеха которой зависит судьба социализма, нашей Родины, каждого из нас.

Я обращаюсь к вам, товарищи, и вашей сознательности и ответственности, к вашему благоразумию. Отсюда и в этом испытании наш советский интернационализм, непоколебимую веру в то, что только в дружной семье всех наших народов мы можем обеспечить прогресс нашего общества, благоденствие всех его граждан.

Я призываю вас проявить гражданскую зрелость и выдержку, вернуться в нормальное русло жизни и труда, соблюдать гражданский порядок.

Наступил час разума и трезвых решений.

М. ГОРБАЧЕВ.

ДРУЖБА—ИСТОЧНИК НАШЕЙ СИЛЫ

Горячий отклик у сумгаитцев, как и всех трудящихся нашей республики, вызвало Обращение Генерального секретаря ЦК КПСС М. С. Горбачева к трудящимся, и народам Азербайджана и Армении. Тысячи людей слушали его позавчера в рабочий полдень, обсуждали на

работе и дома, с коллегами и друзьями в ходе минувшей Ленинской пятницы.

Буквально несколько часов после того, как было напечатано Обращение Михаила Сергеевича Горбачева, в редакцию стали приходить люди. Люди из разных национальностей, раз-

ных возрастов и профессий, но всех их объединяло одно: взволнованность происходящими событиями в Нагорном Карабахе. Призыв проявить гражданскую зрелость и мужество, отстоять наши интернационалистские убеждения, каждый из них почитал обращенным к себе. Вот и

пришли они поделиться чувствами и мыслями, которые вызвали у них события в НКАО. Об этом пишет Генеральный секретарь ЦК КПСС. Сейчас самое главное, подчеркивают они, сосредоточиться на преодолении сложившейся ситуации.

Читайте об этом на 3-й стр.

The Lowlands of Highland Politics: Nagorno-Karabagh

In the six syllables that make up Na-gor-no Ka-ra-bakh, you have all three empires vying for influence in the Caucasus combined: the Ottoman, the Persian and the Russian. It is perhaps the most condensed demonstration of power and language this side of the Volga: one large (and often waning) empire for every two syllables. The name literally means highland, 'nagorni', in Russian, and black garden, 'karabagh', in Turkic-Persian. A mash-up of names that sit so well together one could almost forget the pulverising destruction that has pock-marked the disputed land between the Armenians and Azeris for according to some estimates, as many as nineteen centuries.

Armenian:
Լեռնային Ղարաբաղի
Հանրապետություն
transliterated Lernayin
Gharabagh

Azerbaijani:
Dağlıq Qarabağ
(mountainous Karabakh)
or Yuxarı Qarabağ
(upper Karabakh)

Russian:
Нагорный Карабах,
transliterated Nagorniy
Karabakh

French:
Haut Karabakh

Anti-Armenian illustration from Karny op cit.

A 113-year old refuge from the village of Vaghuhas of Mardakert region in the background flying missiles. From *Shushi - The City of Tragic Fate*, Amaras, Yerevan, 1997

Blown-up bridge between Shusha and Agdam from *Garabagh, Real History, Facts, Documents* by Yagub Mahmudov, Karim Shukurov, Tahsil Publishing House, Baku, 2005

Today Nagorno-Karabagh counts itself one of the many frozen conflicts riddled across the former Soviet Union. Officially recognised as the territory of Azerbaijan, the area has been run by a de-facto autonomous government reporting to Armenia. We have come to see that the higher the peaks, the harder you fall. Otherwise, how does one begin to explain the dangerous calculation of distinctness + destruction + determination characterising the mountain politics of a place like Shusha, the historical capital of Nagorno-Karabagh? Renowned as a cultural centre in the South Caucasus, Shusha's name itself, meaning 'glass', denotes a decidedly Eurasian approach to those ideas typically considered the domain of the 'white man' – i.e. enlightenment, transparency, pluralism. A city where intellectuals, writers, and musicians gathered, Shusha was even known as the 'musical conservatory of Transcaucasia'. We can only hope that the present-day divide between Armenians and Azeri was dealt with with more delicacy in the late-eighteenth century than it is today. Shusha used to be the capital of the Karabagh Khanate, a relatively successful independent Turkic-Persian province (1747 – 1805), until its conquest first by the Persians and by then the Russians, who dissolved any hint of sovereignty quicker than a cube of sugar in a cup of hot tea.

The tombstone bust and sarcophagus of Vagif inside the mausoleum following four images from *Shushi – Mausoleum of Panah Vagif* by Mamed-Zadeh, Elm Publisher, Baku, 1986

Vagif's poetry festival

Heydar Aliyev at the opening of the Mausoleum of Molla Panah Vagif, Shusha, 1982

The prose of conquest / the poetry of arms A man of letters as well as a man of the state, Vazir – or minister of Foreign Affairs of the Karabakh Khanate – Molla Panah Vagif (1717 – 1797) had a way with words. As the founder of Azeri realism, Panah Vagif wasn't like the flowery lyricists of previous generations but rather the straight and simple slugger of a pre-modern era. In a famous episode of royal beef that took place during the 1795 siege of Shusha in the fortressed capital of the Karabakh Khanate, the Persian Shah Agha Mohammad (1742 – 1797)[1] sought a poem from Urfi (c. 1560 – 1592), a Persian-Indian poet, who in many ways was the antithesis of Panah Vagif, to accompany an arrow shot over the city walls.

[1] Shah Agha Mohammed, or Muḥammad Khān Qājār, established the Qajar dynasty. He moved the capital to Tehran to keep an eye on the encroaching Russian influence in the Caucasus. Particularly known for bringing a unity to Persia unseen since the Safavids, Shah Agha Mohammed could be extremely violent, massacring some 20,000 – 40,000 Georgians in 1795 in particular.

ز منجنیق فلک سنگ فتنه می بارد
توابلهانه گریزی به آبگینه حصار؟

Lunatic! A hail of stones descend from the Catapult of heavens, while you await wonders in walls of glass?

When Ibrahim Khalil Khan (1730 – 1806), the ruler of Shusha, received it, he most likely tried to avoid a smile at Urfi's characteristic linguistic play, using *shisha*, *glass* in Azeri and Farsi. He summoned Vagif, his Vazir, who swung back:

گرنگهدار من انست که من میدانم

شیشه را در بغل سنگ نگه میدارد

If my protector is the one that I know,
[he] would protect the glass alongside the most solid stone.

Panah Vagif's riposte proved accurate, as the Qajar Shah of Iran abandoned his siege after thirty-three days.

Mausoleum of Molla Panah Vagif before the Nagorno-Karabagh war *(left)*

Persian Shah Agha Mohammad iranchamber.com *(above)*

For quite some time, I have benefited from a kind of pan-immigrant look, or what I call the 'third-world skin / first-world passport' phenomenon. The first-world passport offers access to pretty much any country but the safety from small (theft) or larger (kidnapping) crimes are the benefits of having third-world skin, looking like an immigrant, or simply, by negation, *not* looking like you have that first-world passport somewhere tucked away.

The one instance I couldn't 'pass' was, strangely, as an Armenian in Tehran. This was particularly frustrating given that Armenians are perhaps the most physiognomically similar peoples to Iranians. If you like a tipple in a country where alcohol is prohibited, the real underground find is the Armenian social club in Tehran.[2] I thought a trip to the Armenian capital would shed some light on why those who looked so similar to me made me feel so distant.

Whoever said 'It's not where you're from, it's where you're at' clearly wasn't from Yerevan, the Armenian capital. No matter how illustrious your immigrant origins, be they Persian, Hellenic, Egyptian or other, they do not hold water to that of a diaspora. Armenians are, along with the Jews, one of only a few exemplary diaspora peoples of the world. And, fittingly, they have been known throughout history for their trading skills, initiating a proto-globalisation as it were:

Youth's Palace 1970

View of Mt. Ararat

Tsitsernakaberd Memorial, Museum of the Armenian Genocide

a network stretching from South America to East Asia dating as far back as the fourteenth century, following the loss of Armenian statehood. But with this illustrious history comes the heavy weight of origins.

The capitals of neighbouring Georgia and Azerbaijan, Tbilisi and Baku respectively, were for long stretches of time the home to significant populations of Armenians.[3] A rich lexicon designating where an Armenian is *from* does nothing to mitigate a sense of loss inevitably enveloping this otherwise sleepy city. At the top of the pyramid are the *Hayastantsis*, those residing in the motherland, then there are, among others, the *Parskahays*, those residing in present-day Iran, and the *Lipananahays*, in Lebanon.

If Yerevan is a capital in the way that Tehran may be – as in, *a head* – I can't help but feel the acephalic culture that makes up the Armenians is *very* far away.[4] As large communities prosper in Paris, Glendale, Tehran, and Moscow, Yerevan struggles to match the cosmopolitanism of its very people. To be fair, the diaspora Armenians have poured money into the country and the capital but, ironically, their successful integration abroad has made a return all the more unlikely. History for the Armenians clearly happens elsewhere as the city has become an urban personification of Tom Wolfe's famous line – 'You can never go home'. According to rough estimates, eight million Armenians live abroad while only three million live in Armenia. Even the omnipresent national landmark – Mount Ararat – is somewhere else, across the borders in East Turkey.

The political equivalent of David Addison and Maddie Hayes of *Moonlighting*, Russia and Iran are today akin to the bickering duo who accidentally find themselves in bed together one morning.[5] Caught between these unforgiving juggernauts with bipolar swings of receding and resurgent confidence, Armenia provides the sheets in between: a soft but ultimately fragile prop. The loss of Yerevan's innocence coincides with a realpolitik gamble that has placed the city on a new axis, one that is a departure from its westward-looking aspirations.

Today, Yerevan stands in step with Tehran and Moscow – the capitals, respectively, of my national heritage and my adopted nation – in an axis as heavy with history as the competing axis (Tbilisi, Baku, Ankara, Washington) is easy with opportunity.

Cascade that leads up to the 50th Anniversary of Soviet Armenia Monument

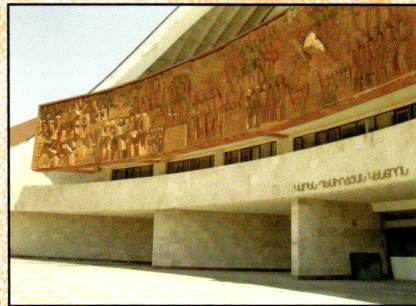

Sports and concert complex entrance

Sports and concert complex general view

[1] *A Radical Reformer, i.e. a Neck or Nothing Man! Dedicated to the Heads of the Nation* was the title of an 1819 George Cruikshank caricature in which a fire-breathing, guillotine-shaped monster terrorises British leaders.

[2] The Zoroastrian, Jewish, and Christian Armenian community are exempted from the alcohol prohibition due to their faith. Nonetheless, identification within these communities is strictly enforced when there is alcohol present to avoid allowing access to Muslims.

[3] After the Persian destruction of Tbilisi in the nineteenth century, the present-day Georgian capital had a majority Armenian population due to the Tsars' repatration of Armenians following the Treaty of Turkmenchay. Furthermore, in the early twentieth almost half of Yerevan's population was Azeri. See *Russian History Encyclopedia*, Gale Group November 2003.

[4] Acephalous, from the Greek *akephalos* (from a- + kephal, head), means literally 'headless', an acephalous society being one that lacks a leader. *Acéphale* was also the name of a publication of a secret society initiated by Georges Bataille, the French philosopher, between 1936 and 1939.

[5] Historical enemies for influence in the region, Russia and Iran have found themselves current allies due to a growing U.S. presence in the region, seen as a threat to their national interests. Nasib L. Nassibli, 'Azerbaijan-Iran Relations: Challenges and Prospects (Event Summary)'. Kennedy School of Government, Harvard University. Cambridge, MA.

Last of the Eurasianists, 2008
screenprint, 70×100
cm

'I AM THE LAST OF THE EURASIANISTS' — *Lev Gumilev*

Caucasian Albania

If you pick up a copy of Strabo's *Geography*, the seventeen-volume work devoted to all the lands and peoples known to the first-century Greek geographer, you'll find excerpts discussing and comparing the Iberians to the Albanians. You'd be forgiven for imagining a loose association between peoples living in the Balkans and those in the Mediterranean, even today. In fact, Caucasian Albania was a kingdom of twenty-six tribes (and twenty-six different languages, naturally) that united shortly before the birth of Christ. To rescue a precedent of trans-Caucasian solidarity, one must sometimes go back in time for inspiration. Caucasian Albania provides many such transversal phenomena: it was in present-day Azerbaijan, fell under strong Armenian cultural influence, and had an alphabet of 52 letters, also conceived by Saint Mesrob Mehstots. The language was spoken until the tenth century and a remnant is believed to be in use today by 8,000 or so Udi people in the North-East Caucasus.

Iberia, on the other hand, refers to the Georgian kingdom of Kartli, which existed between the fourth century BC and the fifth century AD in present-day southern and eastern Georgia. The Greeks and Romans simply referred to the area as Iberia, as opposed to the western Iberian Peninsula where modern-day Spain and Portugal are located.

There are several theories that suggest an ethnic link between the Caucasian Iberians and say Basques in northern Spain, but the documentation is inconclusive. Both Iberias though do share a geographic location on the extremities of Europe, east and west respectively. The moonlighting names only add fuel to the fire of meaning – be it spurious, credible or aspirational – already burning in the area.

Caucasian Albania
until 387 AD
wikipedia.org

The Kingdom of
Caucasian Albania
until 387 AD

Camels, 2008,
platinum prints, 30 x 45
cm (each)

The Caucasus is a Man Its Body is ~~Without~~ *Only* Curves

Komitas at G.Bashindjaghian's studio komitas.am

Komitas by G.Khanjian, komitas.am

Komitas Vardapet A musician who sinks into silence is a sight better not seen. Born Soghomom Soghomonyan, the young musician became a monk in 1890 and adopted the title Vardapet, meaning Priest, and the name Komitas in honour of the eighth-century poet. Responsible for introducing hitherto little-known Armenian music to a European audience and preserving a fragile musical heritage under siege, Komitas was rounded up in Constantinople by Turkish officials along with other well-known members of the Armenian intelligentsia on day one of the contested Armenian genocide, 24 April 1915. He was released after the intervention of several prominent figures, but on his return to the capital found his manuscripts destroyed. Komitas never recovered from the attack. Retreating into himself, his mental health deteriorated greatly, and Komitas would spend his final twenty years in a psychiatric hospital in an asylum in Villejuif, outside Paris. He did not die in the Armenian genocide, so much as he died from it.

> *No, now I sing only to myself,*
> *and I sing very quietly.*

From the *Pantheon of Broken Men and Women,* 2008 – present, collage

Sergei Iosifovich Parajanov
Sergis Hovsepi Parajanyan
Սարգիս Հովսեփի Փարաջանյան
სერგეი სერგო ვანაჯანვე
СЕРГЕЙ ИОСИФОВИЧ ПАРАДЖАНОВ
(1924–1990)

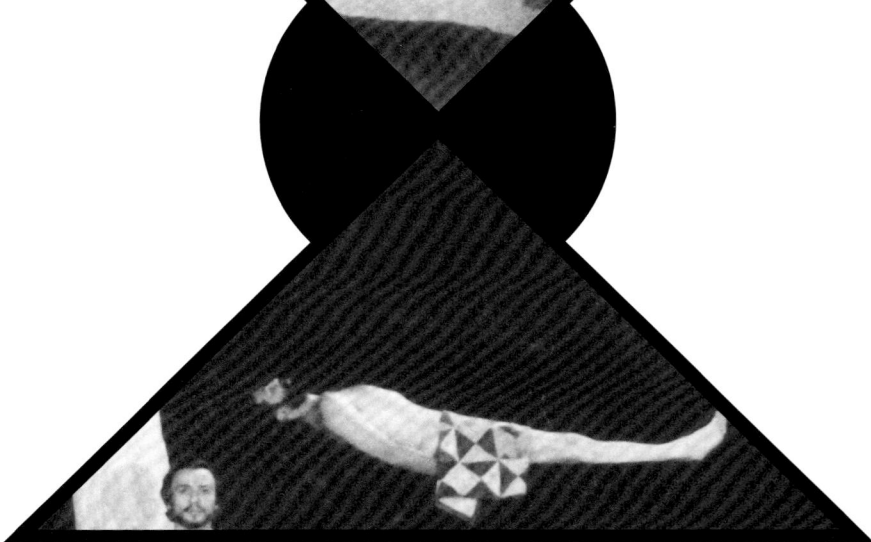

Sergei Iosifovich Parajanov If a picture is worth a thousand words, when an image upsets, does it upset exponentially? In the former USSR, text and image both seemed to rile the authorities equally. And although the ferocity of the censors to some degree lessened progressively after Stalin's death, Sergei Parajanov remained that rare thing: the heartbreaking exception to the ruthless rule. Whether it was his homosexuality or his highly esoteric films, Parajanov didn't conform in any way to the tired social realism already on its last legs – neither through his choice of subject matter (national folk heroes in nations subsumed by the Soviet Union), nor his methods (privileging the visual over the narrative).

Arrested three times, his films were continuously banned, either before, during, or after production. His personal life did not help heal the professional wounds: his first wife, Negyar Kiromova, a Muslim Tatar, was killed by her relatives shortly after their marriage for having converted to Orthodox Christianity. Yet in his broad and almost equal interest in local Ukrainian dialects (hutsul), Armenian poets (Sayat Nova, 1712 – 1795),[1] Azeri folklore and Russian literature (Ashik Kerib).[2] Parajanov was in many ways more Soviet than the authorities themselves. Or perhaps, to revise Alexei Korotyukov's remark: Sergei made films not according to what the Soviet Union allowed, but according to what the Soviet Union would have allowed, had God been a Soviet himself.[3]

Lev Nussimbaum Once upon a time in the West, looking like a muslim was cool. It did not stem from anti-Bush solidarity, nor was it solely espoused by dread-head peaceniks. Instead, urban sophisticates would do their best to out-orientalise themselves and thus each other. (A far cry from Martin Amis, to be sure.) If anyone stood out among the richly busy fabrics and busily rich socialites, it was Lev Nussimbaum, the prolific writer, biographer and orientalist known for having reinvented himself under Muslim pseudonyms in interwar Germany. Tom Reiss's best-selling biography of Nussimbaum, *The Orientalist*, investigates the identity of the Jewish author behind Azerbaijan's national novel, *Ali and Nino*. The story involves a young Azeri Muslim boy and a Georgian Christian girl in love against the odds.[4]

The son of a wealthy Jewish Azeri oil baron and a Belorussian Jewish left-wing activist, Nussimbaum himself and his father fled the Bolsheviks to the east in 1917 across the Caspian Sea to Turkmenistan (the gales of history in the direction of his dreams) before heading back west to settle in Germany where Lev's work eventually earned a place on the Nazi propaganda list of 'excellent books for German minds', despite him being an ethnic Jew. His identity was eventually revealed and Nussimbaum was forced to flee Nazi-controlled Vienna for Italy, where he died in poverty at the age of thirty-six.

[1] Sayat Nova (or The King of Songs) was the epithet of Harutyun Sayatyan, a famed Armenian poet who, despite the pre-eminence of religion, wrote romantic and secular verse. Sayat Nova is considered to be *the* Caucasian poet par excellence as indicated by the various landmarks, schools, and works of art dedicated to and named after him.

[2] Incorporating elements of Caucasian folklore, *Ashik Kerib* is a short story by Mikhail Lermontov set in Tbilisi about Kerib, a poor folksinger, who is in love with Magul-Megeri, the daughter of a rich merchant.

[3] Alexei Korotyukov was an eminent critic of Soviet cinema.

[4] See 'Apostasy is a Conversion too' in *Steppe by Steppe*, p. 2.

اللّٰه

Lev Nussimbaum
Essad Bey
Kurban Said
(1905–1942)

From the **Pantheon of Broken Men and Women** 2008 – present, collage

Left panel of **The League of Impatience** triptych, 2008, offset print, 61 x 84 cm *(opposite)*

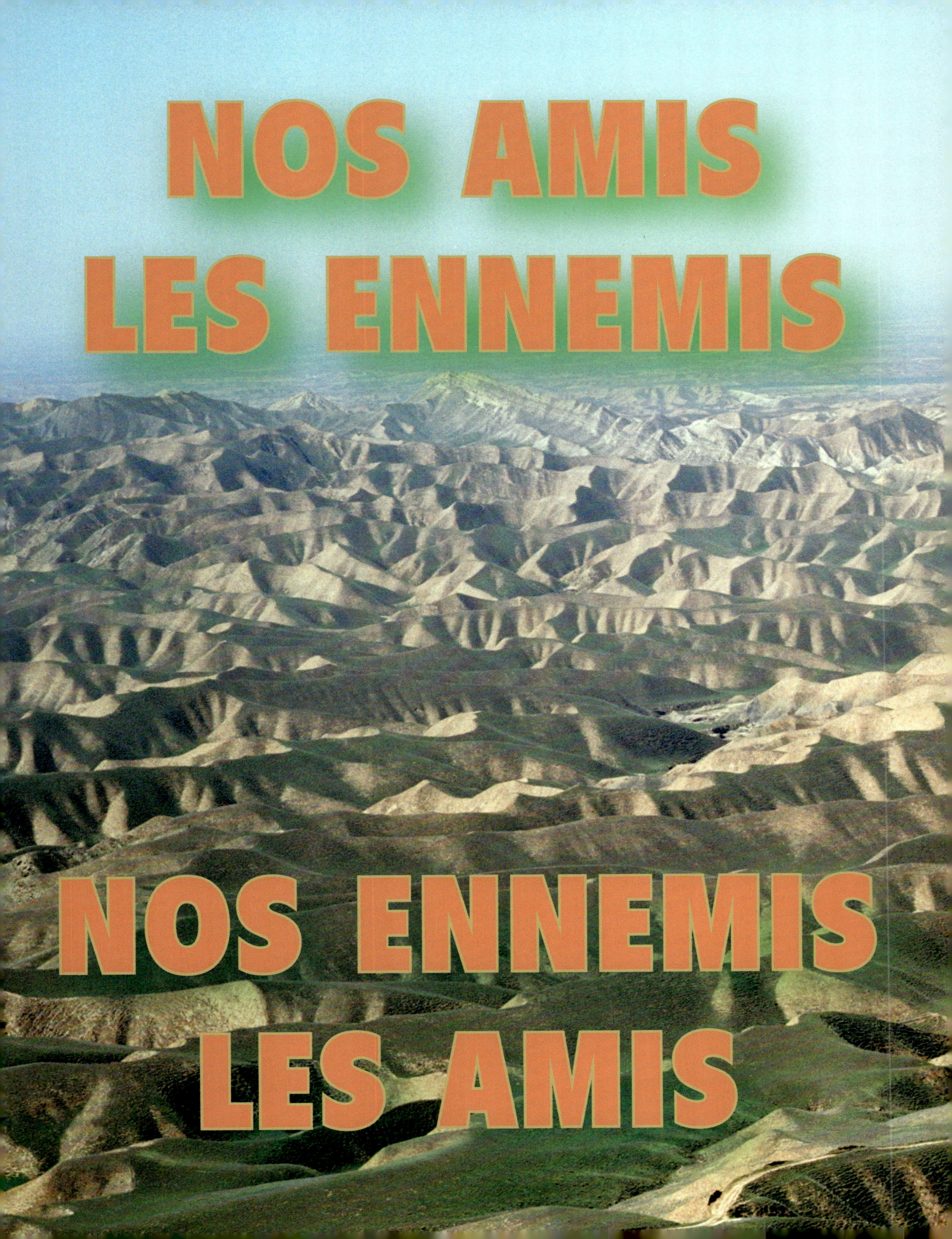
NOS AMIS
LES ENNEMIS
NOS ENNEMIS
LES AMIS

Rossiya two-hall cinema, Yerevan, 1975,
following three images from *Architecture of The
Soviet Armenia* by A.G. Grigoryan and M.Z.
Tovmasyan, Moscow, 1986

Yeritasardakan station
of Yerevan metro, 1981,
(left)

Administrative building
Main Avenue, 1971,
(right)

She's Armenian[1]

Just a   Christi-an girl living in Istanbul Leaving
Where a   mi-no-ri-ty   is a thing most

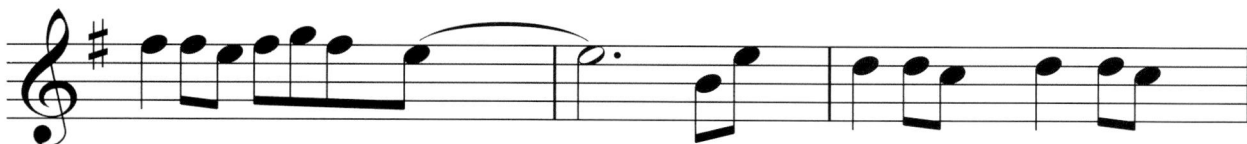

behind her entire life   In the real-time world no one
choose not to see   It's a hard-won place of

sees her at all   They all think she's faking it   Takin' the
tragedy,   touch it, but it can't be yours   You

silver and   leavin' the rest   Gettin' ready to flee into the
run all your life from that moment in time, it could come or pass you

night   She has danced into the danger zone Where
by   Against the push of the Turks, there's always a chance

16

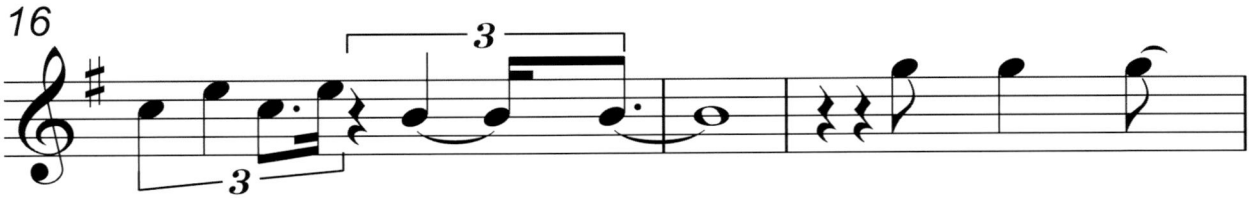

the mi- no- ri-ty is never right She can picture
If the diaspora stays a - live No retreat from

19

the future When Armenians take the stage
recognition without conceding defeat

22

With Agassi,[2] Aznavour[3] and Cher[4] The sights and sounds we've
She'll always be a hay, whether Parskahay or Liba-na-

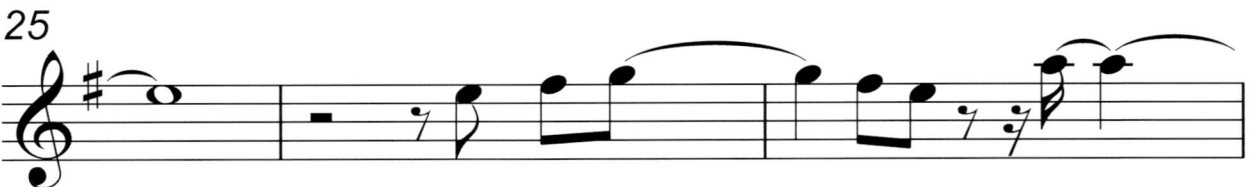

25

seen She's Ar- me- ni- an, Arme-
hay

[1] Based on Michael Shambello's song *She's a Maniac*, 1983, made famous in the feature film *Flashdance*.

[2] Born Cherilyn Sarkisian, Cher (1946 –) is a singer, songwriter, actress, producer, and ex-wife of Sonny Bono. She is the recipient of an Academy Award, an Emmy Award and three Golden Globes.

[3] Born Shahnour Varenagh Aznavourian, Charles Aznavour (1924 –) is a widely acclaimed Armenian-French singer and songwriter. He has sold over 100 million albums and was named Entertainer of the Century by CNN in 1998.

[4] Born in the U.S., Andre Agassi is a former world number 1 professional tennis player of Armenian descent. He enjoys a particular place of pride among the Armenian diaspora around the world.

[5] The Armenians, along with the Jews, are considered to be the archetypical diaspora people. Hayastantsi refers to Armenians living in the Republic of Armenia, Parskahay to those living in present-day Iran and Libanahay to those residing in Lebanon.

28

ni - an   on the run   And she's flee -

31

ing   but   the   flight   has   just   begun

34

She's   Ar - me -   ni - an,   Ar - me -   ni - an   on

37

the   run   And   she'll   fight   until   the   Haya-
And   she's   flee - ing   but   Ka - ra -

40

stan - tsi[5]   are   one
bagh   will   be   won

(instrumental
break)

She can picture the future   When Armenians

take Lenrniyan   With Gurdjieff,[6] Komitas,[7] and Atom Egoyan[8]

The world has yet to see   She's Arme -

ni - an,   Arme - ni - an   on the run

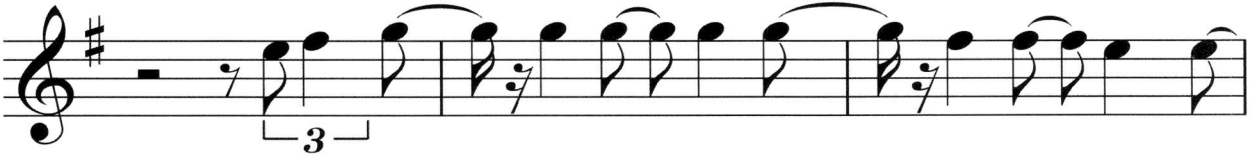

58 And she's flee - ing   but the fight has just begun

61 She's Ar - me - ni - an,   Arme -

64 ni - an   on the run   And she'll fight

67 un - til   re - cog - ni - tion is won

6 A Greek-Armenian Mystic, G. I. Gurdjieff (1866 – 1949) was perhaps one of the twentieth century's most renowned spiritual leaders. He was the founder of the Institute for the Harmonious Development of Man, first in Tbilisi then in Paris. His *Meetings with Remarkable Men* (first published in 1963) and *Life is Only Real Then, When 'I Am'* (first published in 1974) propounded work on oneself and a 'Fourth Way' to bring people to consciousness and otherwise out of their hypnotic sleep.

7 See page 61.

8 Four-time Cannes winner and Oscar-nominated, Atom Egoyan (1960 –) is an eminent Armenian-Canadian director of independent cinema whose films deal with themes as diverse as mourning (*The Sweet Hereafter*, 1997), sexuality (*Exotica*, 1994) and notably the Armenian genocide (*Ararat*, 2002).

NATO
Nanny Approach To Others

In the land of Slavs and Tatars, children are not segregated from their parents. The notion that a child needs to be somehow protected from adult behaviour or language only leaves the child less interesting, if not less articulate. The young Slav, Caucasian, or Central Asian strikes others as precocious, defying the oft-mistaken assumption that going fast means growing fast. We want our five-year old to be brash, resourceful, and prone to using the subjunctive or words *du jour* such as 'sovereign democracy', 'sub-prime', or the prefix 'demi'.

Our approach to education is a disarming one: bring your children to all events, where they walk at the knee-height of adults equally drunk on alcohol and ideology, and where there's not a 'kid's table' in sight. Like Babak Ahmed Poor in Abbas Kiarostami's *Where is the Friend's Home* (1997), who goes on an epic journey to return a notebook to a friend, young Slavs and Tatars go to the great lengths of their little fists, full of immanence and naïveté.

Adorning the otherwise bare interiors of the INFORMATION CENTER ON NATO are children's elaborations on an otherwise particularly adult theme. Rarely does the shiny metal sign disappoint. At the Center, a coterie of young long-legged Georgian women greets you upon entrance, as if to offset the otherwise cold, make-shift emptiness of the centre with characteristic Caucasian warmth. Framed, twelve drawings in all, one for each western calendar month, some naïve, others from the hands of clearly precocious geopolitical pundits to be, aged six to ten. The drawings' theme is Georgia's campaign to join NATO. Why should we spare our kids a crash-course in complexity? They are elastic thinkers, torn between the rules of recess and realpolitik.

Nika Prangishvili, Tbilisi, 5th grade *(top opposite)*

Natia Rukhadze, Tbilisi, 7th grade *(bottom opposite)*

Tornike Abuashvili, Tbilisi, 5th grade

Beviled, Brutal Bling

The mirror mosaics found across royal residencies and Shi'ite shrines in Iran are a further example of the various religious and cultural means employed historically by Iranians to distinguish themselves from Arabs. The highly geometric patterns themselves originate from North Africa and came to present-day Iran with the seventh-century Arab conquests. The Persians, however, insisted on executing them in a more outlandish, precious manner, employing mirrors instead of wood or ceramics. Such an act of distinguishing and defining oneself (vis-à-vis the Arabs) across the decorative arts followed a similar movement in religious doctrine, culminating in the Safavid Dynasty's official embrace of the Shi'a faith (vis-à-vis the Sunni faith of the Arabs and Ottomans).

Resist Resisting God

Defiance in front of divinity is so delectable it requires a certain fierce intelligence, at least as a starter, if not as the main dish.

For the West, it was Prometheus who stole fire from Zeus and gave it to the mortals, and whose punishment was to be chained to a mountain, which happened to be in the Caucasus, his liver being eternally torn out by the beak of an eagle.

Prometheus on the Rock by Elsie Russell, 1994, parnasse.com *(left)*

Monument of Amiran Georgia, by khalampre, flickr.com *(right)*

For the Ossetians, it was Amiran who got into a rock-throwing match with Jesus. After an enormous boulder hurled past Jesus and lodged itself deep into a mountain, Jesus challenged Amiran to unearth the rock. Amiran did not succeed, and as punishment was chained to the peak of Mt. Kazbek. Amiran was a repeat offender, to use the legal lingo of his foe's followers: the son of a sorcerer, he singled out Christians for punishment. To this day, it is said that his despair and struggle to break free of his chains is what causes the avalanches and earthquakes in the greater region.

Finally, for the Abkhaz, it's Abriskil, who is a paradigm of complexity. An ancient hero, Abriskil killed all men with blue eyes (if ever there were reverse racism, *this* was it), and yet primarily spent his time combating evil for his people. He too competed with a higher being, this time the Supreme God Antsvah, claiming to be able to accomplish all that He could, such as ridding the earth of weeds harmful to the harvest. The apostles had a tough time catching him though, as he jumped between mountainside and seaside with his large bludgeon in hand. They eventually came up with a scheme: spread cow-skins where he would land so that he would slip. Chained to a deep cave for his arrogance, Abriskil warns passersby:

> *Get out! But before you leave, tell me one thing: are the evil still oppressing the weak? Are ferns, blackberry bushes and weed still plaguing the earth?*

75

Resist Resisting God 2009, mirror mosaic, 150 x 100 cm

Libération

11 RUE BERANGER
75154 PARIS CEDEX 03
TEL : 01 42 76 17 89

Dear Abriskil,
It pains us to answer
in the affirmative:
the weeds, blackberry
bushes and many
many more evils still
plague us and the
Earth. The situation
has become slightly
more complicated as
it seems we constitute
one of those very evils
ourselves. On the
brighter side, though,
we do now seem to have
the means to break
through those chains
of yours.

Yours,
Slavs and Tatars

Letter to Abriskil
aka Amiran aka
Prometheus on stolen
letterhead, 2009

S.A.R.L. SOCIETE NOUVELLE DE PRESSE ET DE COMMUNICATION (S.N.P.C.) AU CAPITAL DE 19 080 000 F.
R.C. PARIS 75 B 2357 CODE A.P.E. 221.C SIRET 302 342 365 000 46 INSEE 755370191044001011
CCP PARIS 2240185P. TELEX TELELIB 217 656 F. T.V.A. : FR 89 302 342 365

A dervish once said: between Western Alienation and Eastern Submission I'll take:

a bath

Between 79/89/09 2009, screenprint, 21 x 21 cm.
Image: *The Qaderi Dervishes of Kurdistan*, Kaveh
Golestan 1990, The Estate of Kaveh Golestan

S T E P P E

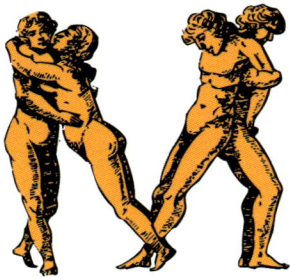  

B   Y

   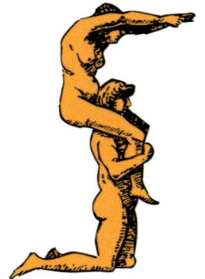

S T E P P E

Steppe by Steppe Romantics. As paradigms come crashing down around us like condemned tower blocks, perhaps we can turn to something that may indeed be broken but is certainly worth fixing. In the twenty-first century, it has become difficult to write earnestly about love. The very term love, and worse, the feeling itself, has been hijacked by hostile forces. It is reproduced, packaged, and sold on the one hand, and, in an equally damaging, knee-jerk resistance to its incorrigible marketing, it is blocked out by a callous cynicism on the other. But love is not an either / or proposition. It is one swimming in 'ands', immersed in an ethical, emotional, intellectual, even sensual maximalism. Ignore the temptations of cynicism and the hollow threat of Hollywood and you will find that there is, absolutely, no wrong way to look for love.

Likewise, love's origins require no apologies. It is, by its very nature, unapologetic – even if the means of acquiring it are far-fetched, unprecedented, old-fashioned, or unrecognised by any institution. No true romantic could possibly claim otherwise. What follows, then, in this romantic spirit, is a lover's encyclopedia of alternative philosophies, strategies and customs, harvested from the examples and histories, ancient and recent, of greater Eurasia. These entries are not intended to shock love out of cynicism's stronghold with the seemingly provocative or even archaic nature of some of their approaches. Rather, these texts seek to reclaim the apparently reactionary, to highlight each method's universality, to breathe newness into the old and to make possible the esoteric. There is a romance to be conjured out of the region's at times harsh history, to be charmed out of sterile facts and documents like the proverbial snake out of a basket. We aim to show, fearlessly, that in the farthest-fetched of fantasies, as in the bleakest of realities, love exists.

Go forth and claim it.

I.   THE TRADITIONAL

Just because a tradition has been around for a while it doesn't mean it can't be of use to us today, or even that it can't be dynamic. Neither the modern Don Juan nor the enlightened couple-to-be need be so quick to flee a time-tested ritual; after all, we can be as spoiled by the past as we can by the future.

EVERY LOVER IS A CONVERT

'Love is my religion', sang Ziggy Marley not so long ago, and whether you share that sentiment or not, it is difficult to deny love's affinities with religious faith – and, likewise, the newly-in-love person's similarities to the spiritually awakened, to the newly converted.

Endogamous religious cultures can approach conversion in marriage in one of two ways: they can either forbid it entirely, and hence forbid inter-faith marriage and assimilation point-blank, or they can mandate it, requiring the conversion of anyone wishing to marry one of its adherents. In the latter case, adopting the religion of your betrothed may too easily become an appeasement tactic, a manner of 'greasing the wedding's wheels' where more traditional families are concerned, a reticent compromise. But what love and religion share in the eyes of history is more dramatic than that. It has to do with passion. And whether surmountable by conversion or not, religion is so often portrayed as an obstacle to romance that we tend to overlook all that love and religious conviction have in common.

Because marrying out of love is a conversion in itself of sorts. It involves a faith in the longevity of the arrangement – as with religion, in its very eternity. It implies not only a lifestyle change, but a change in name, in identity, in the make-up of one's extended family – in a sense, of one's entire cultural identity and people. With this in mind, it's interesting that 'conversion', according to the *Oxford English Dictionary*, is related to 'revolution'.[1] Indeed, no mere adjustment or modification, but a revolution, a turning away in pursuit of a kind of opposite; of the righteous path instead of the wrong one, or of the path walked hand in hand as two, instead of the path walked alone. Love, after all, is a divine thing, even between two mortals.

APOSTASY IS CONVERSION, TOO

Lev Nussimbaum, a Jewish writer born in pre-revolutionary Baku, is known to have reinvented himself as a Muslim in Weimar Germany. Although he engaged in some inter-faith romances of his own, Nussimbaum's contributions to the practice come not so much from his own actions, as from his romantic novel *Ali and Nino*, which he penned under one of his Muslim pseudonyms, Kurban Said.[2] The work's protagonists – Ali, a noble Azerbaijani Muslim boy, and Nino, a Georgian Christian girl with whom he falls in love – enter a kind of apostasic engagement, the product of a combination of love, cultural contradiction, and the Russian Revolution. Ali turns his back on his own tradition when he spares and later marries Nino, despite her having been abducted by another man. Nino, in turn, moves with him to Tehran but misses her western freedoms there. The couple dwells in a purgatory of compromise and mutual dissatisfaction between East and West until they are drawn back to their respective sides of that global coin as if by the force of fate: Nino fleeing to Georgia with their child, as Ali perishes defending the Azeri city of Ganja from the advancing Bolsheviks.

ARRANGED ≠ LOVELESS

Don't put the cart before the horse.
-English Proverb

Love and marriage, love and marriage
Go together like a horse and carriage
This I tell you brother
You can't have one without the other

Love and marriage, love and marriage
It's an institute you can't disparage
Ask the local gentry
And they will say it's elementary

Try, try, try to separate them
It's an illusion
Try, try, try, and you will only come
To this conclusion

Love and marriage, love and marriage
Go together like a horse and carriage
Dad was told by mother
You can't have one without the other

Frank Sinatra[3]

When Frank Sinatra languidly compared love and marriage to a horse and a carriage, he never once said that the horse had to come first. Sinatra had it partially right: do away with the cart-before-horse proverb entirely, it serves only to warn against reversing the accepted order in things.

An arranged marriage, today's westerner might say, represents just that kind of reversal, a rejection of the enlightened order of things. That's a relatively recent outlook, though, and arranged marriages are hardly just a Far Eastern practice: 'Matchmaker, matchmaker, make me a match', was sung in *Fiddler on the Roof's* Tsarist Russia, while William Hogarth's *Marriage à la Mode* immortalised its eighteenth-century English incarnation.[4] The universality of the tradition in some sense unites the East and the West – if rarely in marriage or blood, then at least in approach. To assume that a prearranged union is doomed or somehow tainted is to forget that love has no sense of order, however enlightened or liberated. It is to domesticate love, which is better off left untended like the *equus ferus* of the Central Asian steppes.[5] Carriage or no carriage, love is a strong steed, and it can push as well as it can pull.

SECRET MARRIAGE

By their very nature secret practices are, being secret, generally hard to comment on. Still, we can imagine that the institution of secret marriage must be at least as old as that of the public one, possibly older, in fact, if one is to imagine the birth of 'coupledom' as taking place between two people alone under cover of night. And like marriage at large, secret marriage remains an incalculable part of the institution – and perhaps one of its most romantic forms – today.

If conflicts in the South Caucasus have a tradition of inspiring illicit unions between forbidden lovers, few (real or fictional) relationships to date have been as impossible as that of Artush and Zaur, the two male protagonists in Alekper Aliyev's 2009 novel, *Artush and Zaur: A Tale of Love*. The book tells the story of two men – one Azeri, the other Armenian – who fall in love as children against the backdrop of the recent Nagorno-Karabakh conflict. Doubly separated by the war between their peoples, and the stigma of their same-sex attraction, the couple eventually reunites in Tbilisi, where they marry in secret. An absurdist's subversion of *Ali and Nino*? Perhaps. But Artush and Zaur have their precedents in Armenia, throughout the diaspora, and well beyond that. In this sense, clandestine or unrecognised marriages represent a poignant common ground for Caucasian lovers like Artush and Zaur, and same-sex couples the world over, from the Caucasus to, say, California – whether they be Azeri, Armenian, or of other ethnic origin.

As though to compensate, we celebrate the secret ceremony – gay or straight – not with equal but with greater fervour. Just as a stolen glance is more arousing, a forbidden tryst more urgent, so too is the secret marriage more alive, more keen. Marry in secret in solidarity, in lust, out of an exhaustive need. Marry in secret and do with the heart what the gun cannot: melt the frozen conflicts, be they in Abkhazia or in Glendale.[6]

KIDNAP OVER-HERE,
AND MARRY OVER-HERE OVER THERE[7]

To the men of the West trying to win over the hearts of women who have long been lamenting the death of courtly love, who have futilely awaited their knight in shining armour amidst city lights and bad dates: consider kidnapping. Consider stealing into your future in-laws' home, keeping them at bay at sword-point. Consider the Bactrian camel: your very own dromedary built for two. Consider a honeymoon among the peaks of the Caucasus.

If a man loves a woman but doesn't come from the right family or can't afford the dowry, kidnapping is the consummate chivalric option – an urgent and dramatic take on the surprise elopement – avoiding the at times prohibitive expenses of weddings and bridal fees. Kidnapping is a submission to the anarchic impulses of romance: like love itself, it is criminal, and yet you do it. You do not know how the gesture will be received, and yet you are compelled forward, with the life-or-death urgency of the last resort, of the 'only chance'. The kidnap cannot be duplicated, nor can it be rehearsed: it is the nuclear option of love, if ever there were one. You must sweep the target off her feet with such a strength as to divorce her from everything else in life. If all goes well, you lie low for a while, use the time to cultivate your mutual affections, and return to reality (to the village, and society) as husband and wife. If you fail, lives will be turned upside-down, but such is the nature of love, kidnap notwithstanding.[8]

MY VERY FIRST SHOTGUN WEDDING

Instead of putting a gun to anyone's head, try putting a bullet in their headboard. One Abkhazian matchmaking phenomenon does just that: 'agarafakuara' or 'dissection of cradle', an early betrothal tradition from the fraught nation of Abkhazia, between the peaks of the Caucasus and the shores of the Black Sea.

During the 'cradle treaty' or 'cradle agreement' (колыбельный сговор), the Abkhazians cut notches into the handles of the cradles. The groom's family then fire a bullet into the headboard of the (distant) future bride's cradle.

It's a combination of the world's two most powerful forces – the gun on the one hand, the hand that rocks the cradle on the other – in an engagement ceremony fit for the drama of Abkhazia, a nation still fighting for recognition in the wake of a controversial recent past.[9] It just goes to show that even (or perhaps, especially) in the rockiest of regions, nothing says 'marry me' like a little bit of gunfire. Romantics love violence, too, we say – and nowhere does this hold as true, perhaps, as it does in the Caucasus.[10]

BÖRTE, FIRST WIFE OF GENGHIS KHAN

Speaking of love and violence, Sergei Brodov's film *Mongol* (2008) begins with an episode from the life of Genghis Khan, in which the would-be conqueror, then called Temudgin, was only nine years old. A perfect time, according to tradition, to set out to find a bride, and so Temudgin and his father embarked on a journey to choose a suitable fiancée from the rival Mekrit tribe. The young Khan, however, had other ideas, falling for a slightly older girl from a clan they encountered en route. The young girl, Börte, would indeed become Temudgin's wife, despite his father's chagrin. It was a decision that some historians believe was one of Ghengis Khan's steps on the road to world domination: after they were married, Börte was abducted by the Mekrit. It was Temudgin's decision to rescue her, it is said, and his success in doing so, that launched his life as a conqueror.

If Slavs and Tatars' children are brash, resourceful, and precocious – just like our adults, only smaller – then the nine-year-old Genghis Khan is our number one children's role model, his father's parenting strategy one to aspire to.

Not only did the young Temudgin walk knee-high among adults, drunk on ideology, his pre-pubescent fists up in arms, but he showed that even puppy love conquers all.

TELEGONY

Sometimes, no matter how much we want to resist a certain belief or theory, something about it irks you forward, itching like a phantom limb that you know cannot be there. Telegony is such a belief.

In 1820, the sixteenth Earl of Morton bred an Arabian chestnut mare with a white stallion, after having already bred the mare with a quagga.[11] The mare's offspring with the white stallion bore stripes on its legs reminiscent of the quagga's, so Lord Morton wrote a letter to The Royal Society. His and similar reports at the time seemed to confirm the old Aristotelian notion of telegony, which stipulated that just one encounter with the seed of a male would leave a genetic imprint that would continue to affect the offspring of that female indefinitely, regardless of whom she would later have children with.

We now account for 'telegony' with our knowledge of recessive genes. But in some corners, resistance remains: not so long ago, in 2004, Russian Orthodoxy gave us *Virginity and Telegony: The Orthodox Church and Modern Science of Genetic Inversions*.[12] Telegony, it seems, is back, with a vengeance. Its modern incarnation upholds that not only can a woman's first partner genetically influence all of her subsequent offspring, but also that an adulterous woman's offspring will bear physical traits of the adulterer. There are too many vicious racist implications in play here to even start counting, but as adherents will tell you, the theory has yet to be discounted: the proof being in the stripey legs of Lord Morton's promiscuous mare.

Regardless, there is something seductive in the idea that our bodies have a genetic memory all of their own. Fortunately for the modern couple, telegony's premise is salvageable if used positively. If a woman's core were to keep a souvenir and the potential child bearer played her cards right, the results could be extraordinary: double-conceptions were common among Greek heroes such as Theseus, who was conceived from a mix of both divine (Poseidon's) and human (Aegeus', King of Athens) semen. The child could be a simultaneous embodiment of the personal and collective unconsciousness, of multiple cultural impulses: a worldly, future human being.

II.   THE MATERIAL

E-MAIL ~~ORDER BRIDES~~ ROMANCES

It is true that love as we know it cannot be purchased. Sex, on the other hand, can be – we call its trade 'the oldest profession'. So can companionship, if you're not too picky about it. But what romantics seek is *genuine*, and the cynical pragmatism necessary in the kind of arrangement implied by the term 'mail order bride' would seem deeply at odds with the romantic's agenda: trepidation and the sublime cannot be bought. Romantics are no realists, but that doesn't mean they want to be lied to.

That's why we need to revise our terms. Internet courtships are the new mail-order brides. Girl signs up, uploads pictures, awaits eager replies. Boy logs on, browses profiles, and eagerly replies. The girl's transatlantic passage is nothing more than a marriage pre-arranged by the very bride- and groom-to-be, an agreement between two adults like any other, love-based marriage. Except that this is not lavalife.com, and the long-distance online courtship has not been taking place between Springfield, Illinois and Tampa, Florida, but between the United States and, most likely, a former Soviet state. Certainly, more often than not, there is a monetary exchange. If you're searching for love online, coming from a bona fide western country and having $5,000 and enough for airfare seems to be sufficient. This isn't just romance, it's international politics. And, whoever says romance and politics can't co-exist doesn't know much about either.

WHEN TURKMEN BRIDES WERE UNAFFORDABLE

Perhaps one of the paradoxes of authentic love in modern times is that just because you can't buy it outright, it does not mean it isn't sometimes very costly. Turkmenistan faced the situation of bride-purchasing head-on in 2001, when the country's first president Saparmurat Niyazov passed a decree requiring any foreigner wishing to marry a Turkmen citizen to pay a $50,000 down payment for 'prospective children' – putting a clear price on official permission. The bill was described as an effort to keep Turkmen women out of the harems of wealthy Asians, and away from the abuses and cons of marauders masquerading as rich foreign businessmen. The new laws in a sense hijacked the local tradition of the kalym, a dowry-like payment made by the family of the groom to that of the bride. Instead they made payment to the state compulsory, as though to a collective head of family (an ironic throwback to Soviet-era family politics) through a decree designed to assert Turkmenistan's own national identity.

A wily standardisation of bride prices on the one hand, a nearly insurmount-able act of isolationism on the other. It was like a reversed version of the *prima nocte* we all remember from Mel Gibson's *Braveheart*, according to which grotesque English aristocrats were allegedly entitled to bed newly wed women on their wedding night, in an effort to 'breed out the Scots' (the English must have known about telegony, too). Filthy rich bride collectors and so-called travelling con artists aside, to those citizens of Iran, Turkey, or neighbouring former Soviet republics whose eyes may have caught sight of a beautiful

Turkmen woman from across the border: kidnapping and / or secret unions might be the most prudent, not to mention frugal, way to go.

LOVE AT FIRST SIGHT: SIR SAMUEL AND LADY FLORENCE 'FLOOEY' BAKER

If you can't buy love as such, then maybe it is possible to buy your beloved – especially if she happens to be up for auction.

In the late 1850s, a British explorer, officer, engineer, hunter, naturalist, writer and abolitionist named Samuel Baker accompanied Maharajah Duleep Singh to a slave auction in Vidin, on the Bulgarian southern bank of the Danube. The trip was a *blague*, undertaken for the amusement of the Maharajah. And amuse him he did: there, Baker fell instantly in love with a white slave girl up for sale. He was outbid by the local Ottoman Pasha, but managed to abduct the woman, bribing her attendants and fleeing in a carriage, with a perplexed Maharajah in tow.

The two would eventually marry. But before she became Lady Florence Baker, she was Barbara Maria, daughter of a Hungarian Székely officer, based in Transylvania.[13] She lost most of her family during the 1848 revolutions, and was abducted in Vidin at a young age by an Armenian slave merchant, to be groomed for a harem. 'Flooey', as Baker affectionately called her, would accompany the explorer everywhere he travelled. This included Africa, where she went to the source of the Nile, and where natives nicknamed her Myadue, or Morning Star, on account of her long, blond hair. She died age seventy-four, nineteen years after her husband, on their Devonshire estate. Flooey's almost preternatural, Romanian mobility only made the British come across as more ossified. Lord Baker was never accepted at Queen Victoria's court: she was, apparently, biased towards his wife's origins and the circumstances in which they had met. Still, Lady Baker remains the Sleeping Beauty of the Carpathians, her husband the intrepid knight-cum-thieving Aladdin-cum-Indiana Jones amidst the thorns of the Briar Rose that was the British Empire.

THE BEAUTIES OF CIRCASSIA

For one Circassian, a sweet girl, were given,
Warranted virgin. Beauty's brightest colours
Had decked her out in all the hues of heaven.
Her sale sent home some disappointed bawlers,
Who bade on till the hundreds reached the eleven,
But when the offer went beyond, they knew
'Twas for the Sultan and at once withdrew.

Lord Byron, *Don Juan*, canto IV, verse 114 , 1819 – 1824

If beauty is indeed in the eye of the beholder, then the European beholders of the eighteenth and nineteenth centuries seem to have been seeing eye to eye with Lord Byron when it came to the women of Circassia. Famous for their vibrant, spiralling curls, these women of the North Caucasus were said to be the most beautiful, spirited and elegant in the world. Being the well-travelled rake that he was, Byron would know.

Both Voltaire and Karl Marx mention the Circassian beauties in their writings as well, though the latter not so much for their arresting beauty as to condemn its being bought or sold. A reminder of a darker sense of the term 'beauty industry', these women became a lucrative Caucasian export, both in the flesh, as concubines, and in image, as the faces of skin and hair products, marketed to westerners wishing to imitate their rosy mountain complexion and lush, dark curls. As the Circassians' reputation has faded, along with the cure-all beauty creams and elixirs their likeness was used to sell, so too has our emphasis on the beauty of natural elegance and the 'rural bloom' for which these beauties were known. Today products abound to ease frizz, to straighten and calm and flatten our hair. But calm and flat do not belong to the same vocabulary as passion or ardour, which is why, in an unprecedented instance of product-placement, we would like to suggest the 'Balm of Mecca' to all those seeking to enhance their natural charms to attract a mate, as advertised in the *New York Herald*:

> *This delicate as well as fragrant composition has been long celebrated as the summit of cosmetics by all the Circassian and Georgian women in the seraglio of the Grand Sultan. [...] Any lady must be as great an Infidel as the Grand Sultan himself, who, after receiving such authority can doubt that her skin will become as superlatively smooth, soft, white and delicate, as that of the lovely Fatima, whatever may have been its feel or its appearance before. What fair one but must yield implicit faith, when she has the honour of the Countess De – fairly pledged, that all sepacious [sic] impurities will be at once removed by this wonder-working nostrum. And above all, who but must long for an article, from the seraglio of the Grand Turk, which produces a near resemblance to the Georgian and Circassian beauties?*[14]

III.   THE IMMATERIAL

MAKE BELIEVE IN LOVE

Love, being as intangible as it is, is often compared to magic, that inexplicable, sometimes sublime, sometimes sinister force that we are so often inclined to deny. If only, perhaps, because we resent it, because we feel abandoned or betrayed by it. 'Love is like magic', an irritating, Disney-fied statement, rings true to some because love is intoxicating and debilitating, in a good way. So enchanting that it disables one's own powers of operation in favour of more sublime, more pleasurable ones. To others it resonates because love represents an illusion, because it is in the eye of the beholder, because as soon as one's perception changes, the sentiment vanishes. Or, worse, it crumbles before one's eyes.

The problem with love's comparison to magic, then, is not that it's inaccurate, but simply that magic has a terrible reputation. To 'believe in magic' is to partake in a most saccharine-sounding activity, or, conversely in one of unparalleled abandon, opening the door to forces we've tried our entire civilised lives to shut out: whether they are to do with the occult, the hippy, or the orientalist. It has been simultaneously commercialised for five-year olds, re-branded for the New Agers, and generally rejected by the critically-minded. Not at all for the same reasons it was in the days of witch-hunts and burnings at the stake, but perhaps with the same close-minded end. And yet, that magic's trickiness is somehow bound up in its illusory qualities is somewhat true: its functioning depends on its being believed in. The same is true of love.

For the benefit of love, it's time to reclaim belief.

ON THE QUESTION OF LOVE AND MAGIC BOTH 'TAKING PRACTICE'

'Practice' is something that takes place in the realm of the mundane, of routine and repetition and imperfection, of the rational. Love can be cultivated and relationships can be worked on, but in love, as with magic, after a certain point, you've either got it or you don't. *Practical Magic* is the title of a 1998 Sandra Bullock movie, not a viable approach to the occult. Magic is anything but practical. It involves things like cryptic incantations, tinctures made from rare weeds, moon cycles, menstrual blood, and an investment of the soul that can hardly be described using an epithet more commonly suited to kitchen wipes. Magic is spiritual. It may be hands-on, perhaps, but it is rooted in a deep psychic history that is barely comprehensible. How could such a thing be practical?

'Practical Love', likewise, isn't any kind of love at all. It is, Sinatra might have sung, a carriage without a horse – wooden and immobile. Of course, as far as putting love into practice – that is, making love – is concerned, that is another story entirely, one sometimes as enchantedly impractical as it gets.

THE CORPSE BRIDE: ON DEATH AND MARRIAGE NOT BEING MUTUALLY EXCLUSIVE

Fully related, and second only to magic in the frequency of its comparisons to love, perhaps, is death. It would seem natural that when dealing with the occult and folklore we should find all three – love, magic, and death – cohabiting. Above, you were asked to retire disbelief, or at least in good faith suspend it. But 'The Finger', the tale of a corpse bride that emerged from an anti-Semitic nineteenth-century Russia in which bride murders were as common as Jewish wedding parties, is as real as the Protocols of the Elders of Zion are fake – very.[15] While the original tale emphasised the importance of memory, family, and lineage, our moral is quite distinct: behind every macabre fairy tale romance is a true love story, often gruesome, but sometimes, triumphant.

Once upon a time in Russia (though 'once upon a time' is not appropriate here, as the story is true), a young man who was to be married (and whom we will call Lev, as the characters in true stories should have names) began the two-day walk from his village to that of his betrothed (the names of these villages have changed too many times to be of any relevance). He took with him a friend (whom we will call Sasha).

As the young men made camp on the first night of their journey, Lev spotted a gnarly, finger-like stick protruding from the ground. As a joke, Lev placed the golden wedding ring intended for his beloved upon the twig and danced and sang around it and recited the Jewish wedding sacrament, Sasha laughing all the while. Suddenly the earth beneath them began to shake, as a withered corpse in a white silk wedding dress emerged from where the finger lay. 'You have done the wedding dance and pronounced the marriage vows and you have put a ring on my finger', said the corpse. 'Now we are man and wife, and I demand my rights as your bride.'

Sasha and Lev fled camp and headed towards the village where the wedding was to take place. They went straight to the Rabbi. 'If by some chance you're walking in the woods and you happen to see a stick that looks like a long bony finger coming out of the ground and you happen to put a golden wedding ring on the finger and do the wedding dance and pronounce the wedding vows, is this indeed a real marriage?', they asked in desperation.

A puzzled Rabbi replied, 'Do you know of such a situation?' 'Of course not, it's just a hypothetical question.' Just then a gust of wind blew the door open, and in walked the corpse bride (whom we have not named, her body too decomposed to be identifiable). 'I lay claim to this man as my husband, for he has placed this wedding ring on my finger and pronounced the solemn marriage vows', she demanded, shaking her finger at the groom. 'I want to celebrate my wedding night with my husband.' By this time the rabbi had assembled other rabbis from nearby villages to consult on the matter. Meanwhile, Lev's intended fiancée (we are calling her Larisa) appeared; as Lev told her what happened, she wept, 'I will never be married, I will never have a family.'

After much deliberation, the rabbis reached their conclusion: 'Since you put the wedding ring on the finger of the corpse bride and you danced around it three times reciting the wedding vows, we have determined that this constitutes a proper wedding ceremony. Even so, we have decided that the dead have no claim upon the living.' As the entire village sighed with relief, having lost her last chance at life the corpse bride collapsed in despair, into nothing but a heap of bones, tattered silk, and tears.

Overcome with compassion for the corpse bride, Larisa knelt down and gathered her up, and cradling her close, promised to live out the corpse bride's unrealised dreams. 'I'll live your hopes for you, I'll have enough children for the two of us and you can rest in peace knowing that our children and our children's children will be well cared for and will not forget us.'

With measured steps Larisa marched down to the river with her fragile charge, where she dug a shallow grave and laid the now contented corpse in it, crossing her bony arms over her bony chest and covering it all up with earth, stones, and wild flowers.

Larisa and Lev were married in a solemn ceremony. They lived many happy years together, and made sure that their children and grandchildren and great grandchildren were always told the story of the corpse bride. And so she was not forgotten, nor was the wisdom and compassion she had taught them forgotten either.[16]

SPELLS

'Magic consultations, secret rites, and votive actions', wrote Roland Barthes, 'are not absent from the amorous subject's life, whatever culture he belongs to.' With this in mind we provide you, the amorous subject, with a few spells from the Eurasian cultural region.

Should you find that your spells are consistently unsuccessful, however, try placing a strand of your love's hair under running water in your home. Persistent pressure has a way of wearing down even the most stubborn resistance.[17]

FROM WHEN RUSSIA WAS PAGAN (AND IT HAS ALWAYS BEEN PAGAN)

1. SLAVIC FOR GROW A LOVER[18]

Use this spell to attract a specific lover – presumably, this works best when the lover is somebody who is already no stranger to your doorway.

Dig up his footprint, ideally from your own property.
Put it in a flowerpot, adding additional dirt if necessary.
Grow marigolds in the pot, and your lover will come to you.

2. A DIFFERENT DEAD FISH ANALOGY

*This spell was part of ancient Russian pagan marriage customs.
Its medieval European variant involved putting the living fish into the
vagina and keeping it there until it was certain that it was dead. This less
invasive version should be equally effective, though, in fanning the flames
of passion.*

The bride must be given a ritual bath before her marriage, in that place of
power: the bathhouse.
Her sweat must then be wiped from her body using a raw fish, which should
then be cooked and fed to the groom.

THREE ROMANY SPELLS

1. FOLLOW ME, ROMANY

He may be forced to follow you, but he'll be happy to do it.

Make a paste from your beloved's intimate emissions: hair, saliva, nails,
blood, semen, whatever you've got, the more the merrier.
Mould a little figure from the paste.
Bury it at a crossroads under the first quarter moon.
Urinate over the spot, while chanting: [NAME] I love you! / As this image
becomes one with Earth, / You follow me like a dog follows a bitch in heat
and are one with me!

2. POISON ME, ROMANY

*This is an example of a spell that would seem difficult to execute covertly.
Wine, traditionally, makes a good cover-up for potions involving blood,
ash, or anything conspicuous.*

Burn apple seeds.
Mix the ashes with menstrual blood and add this concoction to food.
Serve to a man to inspire undying passion.

3. ROMANY FIDELITY

*Romany and Russian versions of the ligature spell are identical; who
started it is subject to scholarly conjecture.*

Cut a piece of red silk ribbon the length of a man's erect penis (presumably, specifically that of your target subject).
Keep the ribbon under your pillow.
After making love, take out the ribbon while he is asleep, and soak it in his seminal emissions and tie seven knots in it.
As long as you remain in possession of this ribbon, its knots intact, his fidelity is assured.

3.b SOMETHING A LITTLE MORE MUTUALLY COOPERATIVE

The following is intended to assure mutual fidelity, but also to cement romance, commitment, and partnership. Both partners consciously and willingly participate in this spell.

Both parties must wear a red scarf while making love.
This spell should be cast after moments of mutual bliss. Both parties should be having a mutually satisfying, wonderful time – a true expression of love.
After making love, each person takes off their scarf and uses it to wipe off the sweat from the other person's genitals.
The scarves are then placed one on top of the other.
They are rolled up together and knotted securely at both ends.
They are then placed in a safe place for keeping.
Once a year, the charm is removed – for instance on the anniversary of the spell, a wedding anniversary, Midsummer's Eve, or another significant date.
Do not unroll or unknot.
Place under the bed and make love.

NOTES

1. Conversion, n. (lat. *conversio*): turning in position, direction, destination.
2. *Ali and Nino* by Lev Nussimbaum was first published by Tal Verlag in Vienna in 1937. The story, set in Baku around the outbreak of the Russian Revolution in 1917, is a twentieth-century *Romeo and Juliet* or Central Asian *Layla and Majnun* of sorts. The tale of fraught inter-religious love has been deemed the 'national novel of Azerbaijan'. See 'Lev Nussimbaum' in *Kidnapping Mountains*, p. 63.
3. The lyrics for the song 'Love and Marriage' were written by Sammy Cahn, to music by Jimmy Van Heusen. It was introduced by Frank Sinatra in the 1955 television production *Our Town*, and went on to become a major chart hit that year.
4. *Fiddler on the Roof* is a musical with music by Jerry Bock and lyrics by

Sheldon Harnick, based on a book by Joseph Stein. Set in Tsarist Russia in 1905, *Fiddler on the Roof* is based on *Tevye and his Daughters* (or *Tevye the Milkman*) and other tales by Sholem Aleichem, which he wrote in Yiddish and published in 1894.

5. Like Przewalski's Horse, a rare and endangered subspecies of Wild Horse (*Equus ferus*) native to the steppes of Central Asia. At one time extinct in the wild, it has been reintroduced to its native habitat in Mongolia at the Khustain Nuruu National Park, Takhin Tal Nature Reserve and Khomiin Tal.

6. Glendale, California, which lies at the eastern end of the San Fernando Valley, has the largest Armenian population in the United States. According to census figures, people of Armenian heritage make up 40 per cent of the city's population, totaling some 85,000 Armenian-Americans, while nearly 30 per cent of the city's population speaks the Armenian language at home.

7. 'Georgians themselves, echoing the highland-lowland division among the Scots, defined those who lived to the east of the Likhi as the *amierni*, the "over-heres" in the east, and those who lived to the west as the *imierni*, the "over-theres" in the west.' Stephen F. Jones, *Socialism in Georgian Colors: the European Road to Social Democracy 1883-1917*, Harvard University, Cambridge MA, 2005.

8. А. И. Поршиц, 'Похищение невест: правило или исключение? [Этнографическое исследование]', Советская Этнография, No. 4m 1982, pp. 121-27, Москва, СССР: Издательство 'Наука'.
А. I. Porschitz, 'Pokhishenie nevest: pravilo ili iskliuchenie?', Etnograficheskie issledovanie. Sovietskaia Etnografia, No. 4, 1982, pp. 121 – 27, Moskva. SSSR: Izdatelstvo 'Nauka'.

9. From an 1895 poem by William Ross Wallace, praising the role of motherhood in society, in which he writes: '[...] For the hand that rocks the cradle / Is the hand that rules the world.' The poem's title itself has been adapted to all sorts of meanings, for instance as an example of a social norm gone awry.

10. М. А. Меретуков,'Формы заключения брака у Адыгов', Адыгейский научно-исследовательский институт языка, литературы и истории (Майкоп), Учёные записки, Том 13, pp. 284-385, Майкоп, СССР: Издательство Адыгейского НИИ языка, литературы и истории, 1971.
M.A. Meretukov, 'Formi zakliuchenia braka u Adygov', Adygeyski nauchno-issledovaatelski institut yazika, literaturoi, i istorii (Maikop), Uchyenie zapiski, Tom 13, pp. 284 – 385, Maikop. SSSR: Izdatelstvo Adygeiskovo NII yazika, literaturoi, i istorii, 1971.

11. A now-extinct relative of the zebra.

12. According to 'Woman's first partner may become genetic father of all her kids, telegony says', 27.06.09, Pravda.ru (http://english.pravda.ru/science/health/27-06-2007/94136-telegony-0)

13. The Székely are a Hungarian ethnic subgroup of disputed origin. Often regarded at 'true Hungarians, or Magyars, who were transplanted there to guard the frontier, their name meaning simply "frontier guards".' The Székely form a significant part of the Hungarian population of Romania.

14. 'To the Ladies', *New York Herald*, July 14, 1802.

15. The Protocols of the Elders of Zion is a tract alleging a Jewish and Masonic plot to achieve world domination. The Protocols has been proven to be a forgery, a fraud, and a hoax, as well as a clear case of plagiarism, by respected international scholars, both Jewish and non-Jewish. The Protocols were fabricated some time between 1895 and 1902 by the Russian journalist Matvei Golovinski.

16. See *Leaves from the Garden of Eden*, a compilation of Jewish folktales by Howard Schwartz, Oxford University Press, 1983. Schwartz locates the origins of 'The Finger' in sixteenth-century Palestine, and his re-telling of the tale takes place in the city of Safed. The tale took on a new significance for Russian Jews in the nineteenth century, when anti-Semitic attacks on Jewish wedding parties were on the rise, and later inspired Tim Burton's 2005 *Corpse Bride*. The names and specifics in the above version are the result of our own adaptation.

17. Without inserting a 'don't try this at home' disclaimer, it must be said that: 1) no love spell is a guarantee of anything other than the comfort that the ritual itself provides; 2) while no love spell is a guarantee, the spell's powers are real. Always tread carefully and with respect on magical ground, whatever your beliefs or goals.

18. All the spells in this section have been adapted from *The Element Encyclopedia of 5000 Spells* by Judika Illes, HarperCollins, London 2004.